How Democracy Failed

Ellen Switzer

HOW

DEMOCRACY

FAILED

ILLUSTRATED WITH PHOTOGRAPHS

Atheneum 1975 New York

To Gilbert, Jeffrey, Michael and Kathleen,
who were born and grew up in a country
where we shall not allow democracy to fail.

Extract on page 62, from "Directive" from THE POETRY OF
ROBERT FROST edited by Edward Connery Lathem. Copy-
right 1974, © 1969 by Holt, Rinehart and Winston, Inc.
Reprinted by permission of Holt, Rinehart and
Winston, Inc.

Published simultaneously in Canada by
McClelland & Stewart, Ltd.
Manufactured in the United States of America by
The Book Press, Inc.
Brattleboro, Vermont
Designed by Harriett Barton
First Edition

LIBRARY OF CONGRESS CATALOGING IN PUBLICATION DATA

Switzer, Ellen Eichenwald.
How democracy failed.

SUMMARY: Analyses of interviews with various German
people about national events and attitudes preceding World
War II reveal why Hitler succeeded and the personal reasons
Germans allowed him to come to power.

1. Germany—History—1918-1933—Juvenile literature.
2. Germany—History—1933-1945—Juvenile literature.
[1. Germany—History—20th century]   I. Title.
DD237.S78   943.085   74-19461
ISBN 0-689-30459-5

Contents

Introduction   vii
Important Dates in Hitler's
"Thousand Year Third Reich"   xi
How It All Began   3
Democracy by Accident   10
The Times When Nothing Worked   15
Political Authority Is Derived From the People   22
Paper Money   27
Germany in the 1930s:
"Hate Exploded Suddenly"   44
Hitler   53
Thinking Back   62
Freedom Disappears Slowly   75
"Tomorrow Belongs to Me"   87
What Others Remember:
Voices from Munich and Berlin 1930–1936   93
We Cannot Help Ourselves Anymore   112
The Indifferent Ones   118
The White Rose   124
Dachau Is Also a Town   131
The Survivors   137
Where Was Everybody Else?   149
When Will They Ever Learn?   161
Index   171

Introduction

During the 1960s and early seventies I watched and listened to my two sons and their friends reacting to the constantly changing, increasingly confusing political scene in the United States.

They sat in front of our television set watching the day-long funerals of John F. Kennedy, Martin Luther King, Jr. and Robert Kennedy. Among themselves the young people speculated about various conspiracy theories that might explain the assassinations of these three men. Many of them also cried.

Television brought into our living room the bloody fighting in Vietnam, the tragedy of My Lai, the police riot at the Chicago Democratic convention, burning and looting, combined with police counteracts in Detroit and Newark, the shooting of students at Kent State University and, of course, Watergate.

No one remained unaffected by what he or she saw and read. Some grew increasingly cynical. They stopped listening to and reading anything that had even mild political overtones. They retreated into acid rock, tarot cards, transcendental meditation and, occasionally, drugs or alcohol. Others joined political or religious groups that promised instant solutions, anything from the Weathermen, to Young Americans for Freedom, to Jesus Movement splinter groups. Many wondered why their fathers had bothered to fight in World War II. One evening, after listening to high-toned oratory on "Honor America Day," one young woman said: "Hitler, Johnson, Nixon . . . what's the difference?"

In spite of their cynicism, however, my own sons and many of the other young people who come to our home and who know that I was born and brought up in Germany during the years that democracy there failed, and the Nazi dictatorship flourished, have asked me: "What was it really like to live under a dictatorship?" or "How could the Germans have allowed their government to kill millions of innocent people?" or "Could it all happen here?"

I usually answer that there are a few frightening parallels that any American citizen should watch carefully, and that retreat into extremist causes, mysticism, or indifference for those who will be the future leaders of this country can be very dangerous for all of us. There are still many more differences than similarities between Germany in 1930 and America in 1975. We should be sure that we maintain these differences and stamp out the similarities.

My own memory of the last years of the Weimar Republic and the first Hitler years was obviously not enough to answer even the most superficial questions. I began to wonder what other Germans who had been teenagers during those crucial years had thought and felt. Looking back, might they be able to shed some light on what had happened in their country and why? And might their insights perhaps provide a useful lesson to us in the United States?

So, for about six months in 1972 and for an additional six weeks in 1973, I traveled through Germany with a tape recorder and a notebook, asking Germans, who had been between twelve and nineteen during the years that democracy failed and was almost wiped out in Germany, what they remembered. I interviewed government officials, artists, writers, postmen, railroad workers, beauty parlor operators, waiters, housewives, educators, journalists, anyone who seemed to be

the right age and who was willing to talk to me. A surprising
number of Germans were interested in my project. (It seemed
their children were asking many of the same questions that
American young people ask.)

Many of those I interviewed were willing to have me use
their real names, including some who had been ardent Nazis.
Others were not, because they felt that their stories might
hurt them or their families. In order to be perfectly fair I
changed *all* names and enough details to disguise the identity
of those whose stories appear in this book, except a few who
are so well known that disguise would be useless.

I am grateful to the hundreds of Germans who talked to me
and who allowed me to tape their stories. Dredging up memories of hate, fear, pain, and often, overwhelming guilt, must
have been exceedingly difficult for them. I am especially grateful to one man, Klaus Budzinski, a journalist and writer in
Munich, who helped me to sort out my own ideas, to overcome
some of my fears and prejudices, and who introduced me to
others who knew some of the people I should interview, some
of the places I should visit, and some of the documents and
books I should read. His own memories of the Hitler years
were obviously painful. (His mother was Jewish and he was
in constant danger of being sent to an extermination camp
for almost a decade.) But he felt that my project was worth
the investment of his time and his feelings. Without his help,
this book probably would never have been completed.

Ellen Switzer

Important Dates in Hitler's "Thousand Year Third Reich"

1889	Apr. 20—	Birth of Adolf Hitler.
1914	Aug.—	Outbreak of World War I.
	Aug. 14—	Hitler joins Bavarian Reserve Infantry.
1918	Oct. 13—	Hitler is gassed and hospitalized; goes hysterically blind.
	Nov. 11—	World War I ends.
1919—		Hitler makes first important speech in Hofbrahaus *Keller* (a beer cellar), marking the beginning of his political career.
1920	Aug. 8—	Hitler names his organization the National Socialist German Workers Party; by summer of 1920, it has 3,000 dues-paying members.
1923	Nov. 8–9—	Hitler and a few of his followers attempt a government takeover in Bavaria.
1923–1925—		Hitler is arrested, tried and sentenced to Landsberg prison. There he wrote *Mein Kampf*, which outlined his philosophy and program.
1925	July 18—	*Mein Kampf* is published.

1930 Feb. 23— Horst Wessel dies, huge funeral procession draws attention to Hitler and his followers. Horst Wessel song becomes official anthem of Nazi party.

1931— Unemployment reaches the 5 million mark.

1932 Mar. 13— Hindenburg fails to win majority in election for Presidency.

Aug. 6— General election in which National Socialists win 230 seats in Reichstag.

Aug. 13— Hindenburg contemptuously rejects Hitler's request to be appointed chancellor.

Nov. 6— New elections held. Nazis *lose* 34 seats.

Nov.–Dec.—No leader for a stable government can be found. Several cabinets fall.

1933 Jan. 30— Hitler becomes chancellor.

Feb. 28— A fire is set, burning down the Reichstag (parliament) of Germany. Hitler blames the Communists. Later evidence indicates that the fire was set on his orders by his followers. The occasion is used to suspend civil liberties under Weimar constitution.

Mar. 5— New Reichstag elections, Nazi party gets 288 seats or 44 percent of the vote. This is the last free election in Germany until after the end of World War II.

1933 May 2— Labor unions are dissolved.

May 20— Un-German books are burned in a huge bonfire in Berlin.

July 14— Political parties outlawed.

Nov. 12— New elections, Hitler receives 92 percent of votes.

1934 Apr. 1— Boycott of Jewish shops is begun.

June 30— "The Night of the Long Knives," in which some of Hitler's oldest friends and enemies are murdered by his orders.

Aug. 1— Hindenburg dies. Hitler becomes not only chancellor, but *Der Führer*.

Aug. 2— Armed forces take oath of loyalty to Hitler personally.

1935 Sept. 15— Proclamation of Nuremberg Laws, excluding Jews from German political, social and economic life, and making intermarriage a crime punishable by death.

1936 Mar. 7— Hitler's troops occupy Rhineland, which under the Versailles treaty had been declared a demilitarized zone. Except for a few diplomatic protests, there are no international repercussions.

Mar. 29— Hitler receives 99 percent of votes in referendum. No other candidate on the ballot.

Aug. 1— Olympic Games begin in Berlin.

1938 Mar. 12— German troops enter Austria. Again, few international repercussions.

Sept. 15— British Prime Minister Chamberlain confers with Hitler in Obersalzberg. Returns to England to proclaim "Peace in our Time."

Sept. 30— Munich Peace Agreement signed.
Oct. 1— Hitler's troops invade Czechoslovakia.

1939 Mar. 14— German troops enter Prague.
Apr. 15— Roosevelt appeals to Hitler for Peace.
Aug. 23— German–Russian Peace Pact signed.
Sept. 1— Hitler's army invades Poland.
Sept. 3— Britain and France declare war on Germany.

1940 Apr.–May— German troops invade Denmark, Norway, Luxemburg, Holland, Belgium and France.
May 15— Holland capitulates.
May 25— Belgium surrenders.
May 28— England and France forced to evacuate their troops at Dunkirk.
June 10— Italy enters war on German side.
June 20— France capitulates, signs peace treaty.

1941 Apr. 6— Germany invades Yugoslavia and Greece.
June 22— Germany breaks treaty with Russia and invades.

Dec. 7— Japanese attack Pearl Harbor.
Dec. 11— Hitler declares war on United States.

1942 Jan. 20— Special conference on "The Final Solution of the Jewish Question." Extermination camps are built and equipped; Jews from all over Europe are rounded up over the next three years, 6 million perish.

1943— German siege of Leningrad. Germany suffers its first major, public setback by Russians.
Feb. 19— Members of German "White Rose" resistance group arrested, tried and executed.
May 13— German troops defeated in Africa.
July 10— Allied troops land in Sicily.
Sept. 8— Italy surrenders to Allies.

1944 Jan.–June— German losses continue.
June 6— Allies land in Normandy.
July 20— Attempt of German generals and their allies to assassinate Hitler fails. All plotters are shot or strangled to death.
July–Dec.— Allied successes continue.

1945 Jan. 15— Red Army invades Germany.
Feb. 4–11— Yalta Conference between Roosevelt, Churchill and Stalin to discuss the future of Europe after Germany's defeat.
Apr. 12— President Roosevelt dies, President Truman is inaugurated.
Apr. 25— Russian troops reach outskirts of Berlin.
Apr. 30— Hitler marries his longtime mistress, Eva Braun; both commit suicide in Chancellery bunker deep beneath the streets of Berlin.
May 7— Germany surrenders unconditionally.

How Democracy Failed

HOW IT ALL BEGAN

"... though one cannot always
Remember exactly why one has been happy,
There is no forgetting that one was."

—W. H. Auden.

For me, the Nazi era began the day my father told me that we would have to get rid of our dog, a fierce-looking but harmless German shepherd, who had never bitten anyone in his life. However, he growled menacingly at anyone in uniform, the postman, the garbage man and the occasional policeman who passed our house on a tree-lined street (called appropriately enough, Linden Allee) in Berlin.

In the past few months our dog had found increasing opportunities to growl. Uniformed men in brown or black shirts, singing aggressive-sounding songs, were marching past our house carrying a red flag with a white circle, centered with a black swastika. The flag we had used on national holidays was black, red and gold—the colors of the German Republic.

When my father insisted that a dog who growled at people in uniform might be dangerous, I asked: "Will those people hurt the dog?" "Probably," my father answered. "But more importantly, they may hurt *us*." The dog disappeared, and I never saw that black, red and gold flag anymore, either.

Three years later I left the house on the tree-lined street, the only home I had ever had, not to return. The name of the street by that time had been changed to "Theodore Fritsch Allee." A monument to Fritsch had been put up on the little park near our house. It showed a huge, muscle-bound young man slaying a dragon. The dragon had a human face, people told me that it represented "The Jews." Theodore Fritsch had been an untalented, undistinguished German writer, whose only outstanding characteristic was his violent hatred of Jews. We packed up a few belongings and came to New York City. I didn't see my home on that tree-lined street again until almost a quarter of a century later, when I returned to Berlin as a reporter to cover the story about the concrete, brick and barbed-wire wall that now split my former city in half. The street had its old name back, but that was about all that remained unchanged. All around were the bombed-out shells that had been the houses of our neighbors. My former home had miraculously survived. It is now an orphanage.

Since then I have talked to hundreds of Germans about their first memories of the birth of the Third Reich, which was supposed to endure for 1,000 years but which actually lasted only 12 years and 4 months. It died under the bombs and guns of invading American, British and Russian armies in a war that Germany had cold-bloodedly provoked, and during which millions of people were killed in a reign of terror and oppression unlike any previous one in history.

Many of the people I interviewed remember, as I do, an isolated, seemingly harmless incident that first brought Hitler to their awareness. If there were menacing overtones in that incident, parents and other adults carefully disguised them. Only rarely were any of the children or teenagers aware of the fact that something had gone drastically wrong in their country. As a matter of fact, many thought that something had suddenly gone right.

For a nine-year-old boy called Klaus, it all began when his parents took him shopping at Berlin's largest department store,

Wertheim's, on a Saturday afternoon. There was a huge traffic jam, he remembers. In front of the store were trucks filled with uniformed black- and brown-shirted men who were heaving bricks, bottles and boulders through the store's glass display cases. Klaus also remembers asking his parents why the police were just standing by watching the whole scene and doing nothing. He reports that his parents' answers were evasive, but that someone, probably his mother, mentioned that the owners of the store were Jewish. Klaus also remembers being much impressed by the performance, and feeling that what those men in uniform were doing couldn't be wrong because, after all, they looked so official. "We had all been brought up to respect men in uniform, soldiers and policemen especially," he said. "Imagine, being allowed to heave all those rocks through that glass with thousands of people looking on!"

Two years later he learned that his mother was also a Jew. This fact cast a shadow over the rest of his life.

For a nine-year-old girl called Rosel, growing up in a Bavarian village, it all began when she was told by a classmate that Hitler "had taken over the rudder." Rosel was intensely interested in the rowing matches that took place regularly on the river near her home. She'd never heard of a team member called Hitler, and therefore couldn't understand why everybody seemed so happy that he had taken over one of the boats. She saw people singing and dancing in the streets, and then went home to find her mother weeping and her father trying to reassure her that "nothing terrible would happen." He was wrong. As a Socialist member of the Bavarian government, he was arrested a few months later. He died in a concentration camp. After her mother died two years later, Rosel left her Bavarian village to spend the next ten years in a state-run orphanage, where she was looked-on with suspicion as the child of a "traitor." "I constantly had to prove I was a much better Nazi than anyone else," she said. "I had loved my father very much. It was difficult to believe that he had been an enemy of my country." Before her mother died, she occasionally saw one of her father's old friends who had been a history professor, but who was now a farm laborer because he had lost his university job. At the time, she couldn't understand what this wise and learned man was doing cultivating potatoes for a living. Now she does. "He used to ask me what they had taught us in school about German history," she said. "Then he'd straighten out the facts for me. 'What they are telling you isn't true, you know,' he would say. 'This is what really happened . . .' " Even though Rosel was very young at the time, she knew enough to never discuss her conversations with her father's friend with anyone. However, one day he just vanished. Rosel was told by her teachers not to ask any questions about him.

Hedwig, who was born in a small town in East Prussia, was visiting in Berlin when her father jubilantly rushed into the room and said: "Now I'll be able to get a job." He had come to the city in search of work and had been unsuccessful. They were planning to return to their home where there was no work either. That night she remembers being taken by her parents to an "unbelievably beautiful" torchlight parade. From early evening till far past midnight, Nazi Brownshirts, Blackshirts, and Hitler youth groups marched in disciplined columns throughout the city, passed under the Brandenburg Gate, singing songs Hedwig had never heard before, sounding joyous and triumphant. She remembers her father saying: "I never thought there were so many of us." Her father did indeed find a job in their old hometown almost immediately. There were several happy years in which Hedwig joined the *Bund Deutscher Maedeln*, went on hiking trips, baked cookies, helped on farms and occasionally marched in a parade. She loved the closeness of the group and the feeling that she, as a young person, really mattered to the fatherland. "My father's unemployed friends had always criticized Germany," she reported. "They said we shouldn't even have been in the First

World War. But my father always stood up for our country. He said we would have won the war, but Jews, intellectuals and other traitors helped the enemy. I had never met a Jew, and I didn't even know what an intellectual was. I just felt that they had to be very bad people to betray the fatherland."

In 1941 her father was drafted. He died in Russia. Her two brothers were also killed in World War II. The town in which she was born and grew up is no longer part of Germany. It belongs to Poland. As the daughter of a man who is remembered in the town as a very early Nazi, she can't even go back for a visit. She feels she would be unwelcome . . . and she is probably right.

Joachim marched in that torch parade that Hedwig watched from the sidelines. He had been a member of the Hitler Youth Group for several years, and considered the regular meetings of his troop the highlight of the week. He enjoyed the mountain climbing, the long, strenuous marches, the bicycle trips, and most of all, he enjoyed building model airplanes. "We were not allowed to build real planes in Germany, because we lost the war, and because the enemies of our fatherland didn't want us to be strong again," his group leader had told him. "Now that will all change . . . We will have the greatest air force in the world . . . and become a first-class nation again. Soon you will be able to fly real planes instead of building models."

So, proudly carrying his torch, Joachim marched in the parade that, to him, seemed to be the beginning of a new and brighter life for himself and for Germany. A few years later he was indeed flying real planes, dropping bombs on Rotterdam first and later on London. He was shot down in flames, his face and hands terribly burned.

While he was confined to a hospital as a prisoner of war, he began to rethink some of his most firmly held ideas. "I had always believed that God was on Germany's side . . . because we were right," he said. "While I was in the hospital, and after I got out to see what our bombs were doing, I began to have some serious doubts about my ability to guess what God really wanted."

Joachim is now a priest and a medical missionary. He's still not sure about what God really wants, he says, but he feels that "He's probably not on the side of the warmakers."

Hans and Sophie Scholl can't speak for themselves—they were executed in Munich on February 22, 1943. Their sister, Inge Scholl, speaks for them. "Hans was fourteen and Sophie twelve when Hitler came to power. They didn't march in torch parades because that just was not part of their life-style. But both were glad about Hitler's victory . . . because to them, as to so many others, this meant a victory for Germany. We loved our home . . . and by extension, our fatherland," Inge Scholl says. "Hitler would help this fatherland toward its rightful greatness, its place in the sun, its prosperity. We really believed that."

Hans first became aware that something was wrong when he was forbidden to sing "foreign songs" in his Hitler Youth Troop. His hobby was collecting the folk songs of many lands, and he had often entertained his friends singing in French, English and Norwegian, accompanying himself with his guitar. Now these songs were forbidden by the Führer, he was told. When he laughed at this weird order, he was threatened with punishment.

As he grew older and began to see what was happening to his country, he became more and more disillusioned. At first, he only seemed less happy than he had been. Then over the years, his family noticed an increasing depression. After a term in the army, he went to study medicine at the University of Munich. His younger sister, Sophie, joined him there. Their disillusionment soon found expression in open rebellion: they published a series of leaflets under the signature of "White Rose," which, one sunny afternoon, they scattered on the campus from a window on the upper floor of the medical school. They were promptly arrested, tried, convicted and, a few days later, executed along with several other students and professors. Few Germans ever thought about the White Rose until after the war; but to those who had become ashamed of their country and who didn't dare express their shame and disgust, Hans and Sophie Scholl became a symbol of honor and true patriotism.

Hans and Sophie Scholl were real people, living through a period when democracy had failed in Germany—and dying because they perceived that failure too late. All the other people in this chapter are real, too. They told their stories in tape-recorded interviews. However, some of the names and identifying facts have been changed at their request.

So, the Nazi nightmare began for many in joy, patriotism, and a sense of new freedom. It ended in disaster for almost everyone. How could this happen to a country that had one of the most carefully written constitutions in the world? How was such savagery possible for Germany and Germans who had been known for their art, their music, their philosophy, their medical knowledge, their humanitarianism? Why did so many people support, or at least not object to, the new barbarianism that had taken over their land? Why had democracy failed? That is what this book is all about.

DEMOCRACY
BY ACCIDENT

" 'The really important thing during a crisis,' says one Berliner who remembers the days of the Revolution, 'is whether the streetcars are running. If the streetcars keep running, then life is bearable.' "

—Otto Friedrich in BEFORE THE DELUGE.

The streetcars did not stop running the day the German Empire became the German Republic. To many experts in government it was the first accidental revolution in history. There was to be another "accidental" revolution fifteen years later, when German democracy turned into Hitler's dictatorship.

But on November 9, 1918, no one in Germany except a few of his close friends and relatives had ever heard of Adolf Hitler. Those concerned with something other than streetcars worried principally about two men: the Kaiser (Emperor), a proud, pompous and rather stupid man, who in spite of the pleading of his generals and the threats of French, English and American government leaders, was stubbornly refusing to resign; and Karl Liebknecht, who looked like a minor post office clerk and was a Soviet-style revolutionary.

While the Kaiser was having his lunch in a Belgian resort town to which he had fled from the confusion and disorder of

Berlin, at the end of World War I, Liebknecht was gathering his forces near the government buildings in Berlin, threatening to march on the Reichstag. Inside the Reichstag, a third man, Phillip Scheidemann, the deputy leader of the Social Democrats, Germany's largest political party, was waiting for *his* lunch: a plate of potato soup. As he told it later, a group of about fifty citizens rushed into the dining hall and shouted that Liebknecht was about to climb to the balcony of the Imperial Palace to proclaim a Soviet-style republic.

Scheidemann decided that such a development had better be prevented—and quickly. He got up from the table, went to a window of the Reichstag, and announced: "The Emperor has abdicated . . . Long live the new! Long live the German Republic!" Then he placidly sat down again, and finally was served his soup.

Scheidemann, a former carpenter, union leader and parttime journalist, had very little experience in government. When he proclaimed the republic, there was no constitution, not even a plan for one. His republic, from the beginning, enjoyed very little support. Although most Germans had come to the conclusion that the Kaiser would have to resign (after all, Germany had lost a bloody, costly war under his leadership, and the winning Allied nations insisted on the resignation as a price for peace), many felt that some sort of constitutional monarchy might be the best form of government for Germany. Among the government leaders who held that point of view was Scheidemann's own superior, the leader of the Social Democrats, Friedrich Ebert. "Ebert's face turned livid with wrath when he heard what I had done," Scheidemann told friends later. "He banged his fist on the table and yelled at me . . . 'You had no right to proclaim the republic.'"

However, with crowds surging through the streets, mobs moving toward the Imperial Palace, the police and the army not knowing whose command they were to obey, and nobody sure of who ruled Germany at the moment, the proclamation certainly could not be taken back. Prince Max von Baden, who headed a coalition that was supposedly running Germany in the absence of the Kaiser, simply handed over his responsibilities to Ebert. "Herr Ebert," he said, "I commit the German Empire to your keeping." "I have lost two sons for that empire," Ebert answered unhappily. But the German Empire was dead. The accidental democracy had been born. That evening Karl Liebknecht, the firebrand revolutionary, quietly walked past the guards into the Imperial Palace, entered the Kaiser's bedroom, stripped to his long underwear, placed his sheaf of party literature on the Kaiser's night table, and got into the Kaiser's bed. Apparently, however, he found the situation too noisy, got up, dressed and went home.

There had been surprisingly little bloodshed, considerably less than on an average night in crime-ridden German streets. A new Chief of Police had appointed himself (he simply walked up to Police Headquarters and announced "I'm the new chief," and everybody took his word for it). Fifteen people had been killed, a few more wounded. The entire "revolution" had been confined to Berlin. Citizens throughout the rest of Germany read about it in their newspapers the next morning.

To many solid German citizens, accustomed to respect for the aristocratic ruling class, the educated bureaucrats and, above all, the power of the army, the whole situation seemed a form of comedy. "Isn't this just like the Berliners?" Johann remembers his father saying, while laughingly reading the story in his Frankfurt newspaper. "Well, at least it should make the Americans happy; I understand they do that kind of thing all the time. The French also change their governments regularly . . . but the kings always come back and bring order. This nonsense won't last long . . . but perhaps we'll get a more advantageous peace. After all, our generals will see to it that Ebert and his fellow proletarians don't sign any dishonorable treaty, and things can't get much worse than they are now."

In many ways the new chancellor, Ebert, shared Johann's

father's views, as did a majority of Germans. He had been born to a poor family and had received little formal education. By profession he was a saddlemaker, and when fewer and fewer saddles were needed, he became a bartender. For a while he worked on a Socialist newspaper with a small circulation. Eventually he became a professional party functionary in Berlin, and proved to be a good organizer. According to some of the people who remember him, part of his success was due to the fact that he was less frightened and suspicious than his predecessors. For instance, he filed membership cards and other documents and kept a set of books. Those who had preceded him routinely burned all their correspondence. He turned the Socialist party from a minor conspiracy into a moderately successful political party. However, at no time did he apparently feel himself qualified to run the German government. What's more, his idea of socialism was to provide better working conditions and wages for workers . . . not to abolish a powerful monarchy.

One of the first men he talked to after his unexpected elevation to the leadership of the German government was one of the top army generals, who conveyed a message from Field Marshal Paul von Hindenburg, the commander in chief of the defeated Imperial Army. Meekly, Ebert asked what the field marshal expected of him. He was told that the field marshal expected the government to support the officer corps and to fight Bolshevism. Nothing was said about prices, wages, working conditions or unemployment. Ebert immediately agreed to do as he was asked, and thanked the field marshal for his good wishes. He also promised to use the army to suppress any left-wing revolution, which he assured the general, "he hated like sin."

A basic contradiction had already been established during that first telephone conversation. The German Republic was to be held within certain social, political and economic bounds at the point of a gun. In a way, that situation never really changed until after Germany had lost World War II.

Many Germans probably would have agreed with Ebert's secret compact. They, like him, felt that the new German Republic was totally dependent on the army and the aristocrats. They also agreed with Johann's father that the situation couldn't get much worse than it was. But it could—and it did.

THE TIMES WHEN NOTHING WORKED

"My imagination dwelt on the war, on the advances and retreats at the front, on the suffering of the soldiers . . . with the ardent sympathies of childhood. I would often sleep for several nights running on the hard floor beside my soft bed in order to be sharing the privations of the soldiers at the front."

—INSIDE THE THIRD REICH *by Albert Speer.*

If anyone had asked a cross section of Germans in the last months of 1918 what they expected from their new Republic, many might have asked for peace with the minimal amount of honor that could be salvaged from the thousands of dead and wounded soldiers, the sacrifices of their families, and the destruction of property that the war had imposed upon them.

Then, few thought about how the war had come about, or Germany's responsibility for its beginning. Millions of Germans truly believed that God was on their side, or if He wasn't, He surely must have been looking in another direction. If the war was lost, there had been some terrible mistake, probably brought about by a few traitors and cowards, and history would eventually prove that Germany had been right all along. Even today, a great many older Germans feel that way about World War I, although they may have a different opinion about World War II.

This was also the official line that they heard from most government officials, all generals, many newspapers, frequently in school, and in university classrooms. Certainly Albert Speer, who was then a youngster, who later became Hitler's Minister of Armaments and War Production, and still later was sentenced to a long prison term by the Nuremberg trial judges as a war criminal, thought so. "In spite of the Revolution, which had brought us the Weimar Republic, it was still impressed upon us that the distribution of power in society and the traditional authorities were part of the God-given order of things," he explained in his book *Inside The Third Reich.* "We remained largely untouched by the currents stirring everywhere in the early twenties. In school, there could be no criticism of courses or subject matter, let alone the ruling powers of the state. Unconditional faith in the authority of the school was required. It never occurred to us to doubt the order of things. . . ."

Even Ebert believed in "the traditional authorities": the army generals, the powerful aristocracy and the former high government officials. So, the baker in Berlin, the schoolteacher in Munich, the farmer in a small Silesian town, the worker in a factory in Essen, could hardly be expected to put faith in the few journalists, intellectuals and left-wing politicians who said that the war had been wrong, that the army had betrayed Germany, and that a whole new ruling class was needed to save the country. Germans generally were shocked when they heard about the surrender terms demanded by the Allies: Germany was to give up all its armaments, including its navy, and all German troops west of the Rhine would have to be evacuated. These terms were not negotiable, and peace could not even be discussed without this complete military surrender. Germany had seventy-two hours to accept the terms, or the Allies would start shooting again.

The leaders of the new German Republic turned to the

authority figures in whom they still had faith: the army generals. What should they do? The generals regretfully shrugged their shoulders and told the civilian leaders that there was no alternative: Germany would have to accept the surrender terms, dishonorable as they might sound, or face total physical destruction. They also persuaded a representative of the civilian government, Matthias Erzberger, to head the three-man commission that would sign the surrender documents on behalf of Germany. As it turned out later, the reason the generals wanted civilians to sign the documents was not that the entire military command of the German army had suddenly become so busy they simply could not make the trip to the Forest of Compiègne, where the papers were ready for ratification in a railroad car on an out-of-the-way siding. The German military wanted a scapegoat: someone whom they could blame for the "dishonorable" action (on which they had insisted). The blame would come later, when Germans who had short memories had forgotten their country's desperate military plight. Then the signers of the surrender papers would be characterized as traitors, weaklings and scoundrels who had sold out their fatherland to the enemies.

Erzberger, who had long opposed the war as useless and fruitless, fitted the "defeatist" image perfectly. He was received by the commander in chief of the German Armed Forces, Paul von Hindenburg, before going on his sad trip. According to one journalist, Hindenburg "clutched Erzberger's hand with tears in his eyes and urged him to do his patriotic duty," i.e., sign those surrender documents. Hindenburg, however, said nothing in Erzberger's defense when he was attacked mercilessly by right-wing politicians and newspapers only a few years later for deliberately "losing the war" almost single-handedly. The unfortunate civilian leader was shot in the shoulder by an overwrought young man inflamed by these accusations, lost his cabinet post, and spent the rest of his short life (one year) trying to reestablish his honor.

If the surrender terms shocked the Germans, the proposed peace treaty appalled them. Large parts of their country were to go to their former enemies: France was to get Alsace-Lorraine and would occupy all of Germany west of the Rhine. France would take over the coal mines in the Saar district, on which Germany depended heavily for its industrial power. Poland would get Upper Silesia—rich in industry and agriculture—most of Posen and West Prussia, thus cutting East Prussia off from the rest of Germany and creating a "Polish corridor" through the middle of the country. Other smaller sections of Germany would go to various other neighboring countries. All colonies were to be given over to control by the League of Nations. Germany would be allowed no professional army, only 100,000 volunteers, and would be prohibited from keeping, buying, or building any tanks, armored vehicles or planes. The country would be forced to pay reparation (eventually amounting to as much as 120 billion marks) for the damage German armies had done to their former enemies during the war. Along with all these material losses, there would also be a complete loss of face: Germany would have to admit, in writing, the sole responsibility for starting and prosecuting the war and accept complete guilt.

Faced with these horrifying terms, the civilian government again turned to the generals for help. Again the generals insisted that surrender was inevitable. If a signature were refused, Germany would be invaded on all sides, and no strategy that they could devise would save the country from complete destruction. And again the military men refused to sign the peace treaty themselves; they insisted that this was the responsibility of the civilian government. Bowing to authority, the civilian leaders accepted the disagreeable task of signing large parts of their country over to their former enemies and accepting the responsibility for the war. They, too, were eventually to feel the wrath of those Germans who either did not understand their own history, chose to forget it, or could not learn from it. Among the leaders of the Germans who cursed the civilian representatives were the generals who had advised them to sign, but had refused to do so themselves.

Among those almost totally stunned by the loss of the war was a young German corporal, Adolf Hitler. He was in an army hospital suffering from the effects of a poison-gas attack when an elderly Protestant pastor arrived on the scene to address the wounded. He told them that the Kaiser had been forced to resign and flee, that the war was lost, and that their country was now a republic. Although he urged the soldiers to pray for this fledgling democracy, he broke into tears. According to witnesses, Hitler "watched the old man weeping in a kind of stupor." As the full realization of what had happened hit him, he reported in his book *Mein Kampf* (My Battle): "I could sit no longer. Once again everything went black before my eyes, and I tottered and groped my way back to the place where we slept, and buried my burning head in the blankets and pillows."

He was never to forgive the civilian government that signed the inevitable surrender terms and peace treaty. He never could believe that the army, which he regarded as the highest symbol of German purity and valor, could actually have been defeated in battle. Also in *Mein Kampf* he wrote: "It [the army] was the mightiest school of the German nation, and not for nothing was the hatred of all our enemies directed against this buttress of national freedom and independence. No more glorious monument can be dedicated to this unique institution than a statement of the truth that it was slandered, hated, combated, and also feared by all inferior peoples. . . . What the German people owe to the army can be briefly summed up in one word: everything."

Toward those who signed the surrender papers and the peace treaty he directed his bitterest sarcasm and contempt. "Fat Herr Erzberger" and Friedrich Ebert were referred to as "political midgets." The rest of the leaders of the new Republic he called "revolutionary bedbugs." The fact that he would eventually come to power partly by storming at the civilian government, which had been forced to make the best of a disastrous situation by the very generals whom he worshiped, indicates that there were many other Germans who agreed with him.

One of those was a man whom we shall call Johann Herbert. His son, Hubert, remembers those early days when the father returned from the army, crippled and bitter. "He had lost a leg on the battlefront, and he refused to try to use a wooden leg. Instead he rolled around the house in his wheelchair and stormed at the 'bureaucrats and bloodsuckers' who had brought Germany into disgrace. He described the leaders of the civilian government as traitors, to whom we owed no loyalty or allegiance. When I brought home the black, red and gold flag of the new republic (the old flag had been black, *white* and red), he ripped it up, spit on it, slapped me in the face and told me never to bring that rag into the house again.

"He was an early member of the Nazi party and used to attend party meetings in his wheelchair, with his stump wrapped in a swastika flag. He would also roll his wheelchair, decorated with flags, around Berlin streets, distributing leaflets and cursing able-bodied men, whom he called 'war shirkers.' The police never did anything about him because they considered him a little crazy," Hubert reported. "I didn't. I thought he was a hero . . . and since most of my schoolmates ridiculed my father, I spent many evenings with him at meetings, listening to the speeches, singing the songs of the new Germany, where war heroes would be respected instead of despised, and waiting for the great day, when we would get back at our enemies: those in other countries and those in the fatherland. I used to take notes in class on teachers who didn't show proper respect for our country, because I felt that some day those notes might be useful in cleaning out the schools of traitors and cowards."

Hubert joined the Hitler Youth Movement very early. He did indeed turn over his notes to his superior officers and today wonders guiltily what may have happened to the men and women he denounced. He feels that Germany was mistreated at the end of World War II, but despises Hitler as well. "After all, he lost a war too . . . and then he committed suicide, the coward," he said.

A small man, whose face twitches when he talks, he still considers those early days in the Hitler Youth Movement as one of the high points of his life. "Everybody thought I was important then," he adds. "Nobody considers me important now. Perhaps, some day, things in Germany will change again. . . ."

When asked what kind of change he is looking for, he says: "Law, order and respect." That, of course, was what his father was seeking, as he rolled around the Berlin streets in his flag-covered wheelchair. What he got instead may be a tiny part in pre-Nazi Germany history, as shown on movie screens throughout the world in the film *Cabaret*. In that film, which takes place immediately before the Nazi takeover of the German government, a man in a swastika-decorated wheelchair is seen moving through a Berlin street. Hubert is convinced that one of the writers or directors of the film saw his father in the early 1930s. "Well, at least somebody remembered him . . ." he said.

POLITICAL AUTHORITY IS DERIVED FROM THE PEOPLE

"The German people, united in all their branches and inspired by the determination to renew and strengthen their Commonwealth in liberty and justice, to preserve peace both at home and abroad, and to foster social progress, have adopted the following Constitution."

—*Preamble, Constitution of the Weimar Republic.*

"We the People of the United States, in Order to form a more perfect Union, establish Justice, insure domestic Tranquillity, provide for the Common Defense, promote the general Welfare, and secure the Blessings of Liberty to ourselves and our Posterity, do ordain and establish this Constitution for the United States of America."

—*Constitution of the United States.*

The apparent similarity between the preamble to the constitution of the new German Republic and the Constitution of the United States is no accident. Those who framed the German document looked to America's basic law as a model, along with the constitutions of other democratic states. However, except in one important detail, the Weimar Constitution was probably closest to that of the United States.

There were some similarities between the men who framed their country's new basic law in Weimar in 1919 and those who met in Philadelphia in 1787. Both groups of delegates were faced with an already existing country that had been formed or formed itself before a basic law had been drawn. Both groups of delegates were also faced with a number of semi-independent states, whose representatives expressed great reluctance to turn over any of their powers and prerogatives to a central federal government. Germany's provincial states talked as firmly about "states rights" as any governor in any of our own fifty states might today when faced with a federal court order on school busing or equal employment opportunities.

Beyond these superficial similarities, however, there were many very important differences between the circumstances surrounding the birth of the American Constitution and those of its German counterpart.

The Americans had won their fight against King George's well-equipped and well-trained troops—a war no one really expected them to win. They met in Philadelphia in a glow of victorious pride. The Germans, on the other hand, had lost a war that few of them had expected to lose. They met in Weimar filled with the shame and bitterness of what many considered stained national honor. America was truly at peace with itself when the delegates met in Philadelphia. In Germany, internal revolutionary strife was erupting into bloody street fights every day. A left-wing group—the Spartakists—battled a right-wing group—the Freikorps—almost daily, with clubs and old army swords, and finally with rifles and machine guns. Innocent bystanders who got in the way just added to the evening's body count. The Freikorps eventually won the battle, and its members installed themselves as a semiofficial police organization. Led by a man called Gustav Noske, who referred to himself as "the bloodhound," the organization hunted down their old enemies and arrested and frequently murdered them. Among those murdered was Karl Liebknecht, the Communist who had installed himself in the Kaiser's bedroom at the beginning of the democratic revolution. Also murdered was a well-known left-wing woman leader, Rosa Luxemburg. The Freikorps' officers reported that Liebknecht had been shot "trying to escape," and failed to account for Rosa Luxemburg at ail. Her body was found weeks after her death. All the time, the officers and men of the Freikorps were acting on official authority, although Chancellor Ebert declared himself appalled by the murders and ordered an official investigation. Eventually one army private actually went to prison for a few months.

It was against this background that the men at Weimar were attempting to draw up a constitution that promised "liberty and justice" to all Germans.

There was one even more important difference between the two constitutional conventions and the two countries. Americans had fought for their freedom. The citizens of Germany had not gone across the sea to a new and wild land to escape tyranny. Germans had had their freedom thrust upon them, as a price many thought they had to pay for a more lenient peace. They had been taught to look up to strong leaders, to venerate authority, to distrust individual initiative and change, especially when it came to government. For these reasons a fatal flaw appeared in their constitution from its inception. Those who wrote the document thought they wanted a strong president, very like the American model. However, their conception of a strong presidency included a special element: under Article 48 a president would be able to suspend all constitutional liberties and rule by decree. That's what eventually led to the installation of Adolf Hitler, who had not received a majority of the popular vote, as chancellor. It also allowed a senile President Hindenburg to suspend one constitutional guarantee after another, at the urging of this chancellor and other antidemocratic forces in the government. In the end, the Weimar Constitution became so weak and meaningless that no one ever bothered to revoke it: Hitler simply suspended parliamentary government, which was entirely possible under cover of Article 48.

As it was being drafted, however, the document seemed to be the symbol of a brighter, freer future. Its principal architect was not a politician but a professor of law at the University of Berlin, Hugo Preuss. Dr. Preuss was not only a constitutional scholar and a liberal, he was also a Jew, a fact that Hitler never allowed the German people to forget when he excoriated the German parliamentary system. "Must not every true leader refuse to be thus degraded to the level of political gangster?" Hitler would ask, when discussing parliamentary democracy. "And, conversely, must not every gangster feel that he is cut out for politics, since it is never he, but some intangible mob, that has to bear the ultimate responsibility? Mustn't the principle of parliamentary majorities lead to the demolition of any idea of leadership?"

At the time the constitution was adopted, the idea of the "demolition of leadership" did not worry just Hitler, then an obscure itinerant artist. Nor was the concept of the German people as "a mob" entirely his. A great many of his fellow Germans agreed with him. They saw the constitution not as a vital instrument of government, but as a harmless piece of paper that would allow governments to run very much as they pleased.

The new constitution contained sections on freedom of speech and religion, freedom of the press (although with specific provisions to permit censorship "for combating obscene and indecent literature, as well as for the protection of youth at public plays and spectacles"), freedom from unreasonable search and seizure, and many of the other features of our Bill of Rights. However, all these guarantees were apparently regarded as not nearly as important as the laws governing customs duties, the administration of the railroad system, and the ownership of the waterways. In reading the Weimar Constitution (which very few Germans apparently did), the guarantee of the freedoms *that were basic to American law* must have seemed very much like an afterthought. The majority of the framers of the U.S. Constitution had insisted that no constitution should be passed without including the first ten amendments, which spell out the rights that no one can take away from any United States citizen.

Germans who were teenagers during the years of the Weimar Republic often didn't know that their country had a constitution. They were frequently so much aware of law and order that, even when storming a building in a radical, rebellious outbreak, they carefully observed signs that said: DON'T STEP ON THE GRASS. But the whole concept of a basic philosophy that assured everyone of personal and intellectual freedom, guaranteed by government, was foreign to many of those young people who had been brought up to respect authority above all else.

Article I of the present German constitution states: "The dignity of man shall be inviolable. To protect it shall be the duty of all state authority." Most German schoolchildren today can recite that article and know what it means. That may well be one of the lessons the German experience has taught them and may teach others who think about it. A constitution is a piece of paper, no more, no less, if it is not regarded as the foundation of all law.

In 1933 some Germans who exercised "the right to petition or complain in writing to the appropriate authorities or to the representatives of the people" (a right guaranteed in their constitution) were sent to the concentration camp in Dachau. A picture in the museum there shows a sad-eyed man with a shaved head—a lawyer—and around his neck is hung a sign: I COMPLAINED. He took the constitution seriously, and in 1933 that was a fatal error.

PAPER MONEY

"Lingering at the [shop] window was a luxury because shopping had to be done immediately. Even an additional minute meant an increase in price. One had to buy quickly because a rabbit, for example, might cost two million marks more by the time it took to walk into the store. A few million marks meant nothing, really. It was just that it meant more lugging. The packages of money needed to buy the smallest item had long since become too heavy for trouser pockets. They weighed many pounds. . . . People had to start carting their money around in wagons and knapsacks. I used a knapsack."

—George Grosz, German painter and cartoonist in his autobiography, A LITTLE YES AND A BIG NO.

FOOD PRICES RISE 4½ PER CENT IN ONE WEEK, an August 1973 headline in the *New York Post* announced bleakly. Two women in the appliance department of a large New York store were discussing the advantages and disadvantages of buying a freezer. "This inflation can't get much worse," one of the prospective purchasers said. "It's probably the worst price spiral in history." "Not exactly," said the other. "My grandmother grew up in Germany, and she remembers a time when you couldn't buy a postage stamp in the evening for what you had received in the morning for a week's work." "That sounds crazy," the other woman said. "If something like that happened, nothing would be worth anything anymore . . . there'd probably be some kind of revolution."

In a way, the concerned homemaker had echoed the words of an internationally known historian, Alan Bullock. "The real revolution in Germany was the inflation," he wrote.

Germany's inflation began gradually, as more goods became available at the end of the war and Germany's industrial production could not keep up with consumer demand. Also, much of her raw materials went as reparations to the Allies, especially France. At one point the French government threatened to invade because Germany had not been able to deliver 200,000 telephone poles on schedule. The German government's protest that there just were not enough trees left to make the deliveries only brought further threats.

There was a great deal of unemployment, especially among the soldiers who had been released from the army, and Germany's new democratic government was pledged to provide some social services. The only way German economists saw to tackle the problem was to print more and more money . . . which became worth less and less.

As inflation took over, the pace of the monetary decline quickened. In the summer of 1922 the mark was worth 400 to the American dollar, by January 1, 1923, 7,000 marks were needed to get one dollar, and by July of the same year, 160,000 marks. Eventually billions and trillions of marks could not purchase dollars, or British pounds, or French francs. The German mark was worth only as much as the paper it was printed on . . . and the paper was of very poor quality at that.

As people completely lost faith in their currency, they demanded to be paid weekly, and then daily, and then hourly. Factories closed down so that people could spend their money as soon as they had received it. Symphony orchestras and plays interrupted their rehearsals because the artists demanded their money at noon to rush to the nearest store to buy anything that could still be bought with money. They went out with bags full of banknotes (George Grosz's knapsack was definitely not an exaggeration) and came back with anything that was available, whether they needed it or not. According to stories of people who lived through those times, men and women bought shoes in sizes they could not wear, knick-knacks they could not use and didn't even like, twenty-pound bags of salt or sugar they would not be able to eat in years. . . . Anything was better than that worthless paper, which the German government printing presses kept turning out. Soon government presses couldn't do the job fast enough any longer . . . newspapers were asked to help out in getting the printing job done.

"At Ullstein newspaper headquarters . . . officials requisitioned presses to turn out increasingly worthless paper," Otto Friedrich tells in *Before the Deluge.* "All doors [at the newspaper] were locked and officials from the Reichsbank [the government-operated German banking system] were placed on guard. . . . Round the machines sat elderly women, staring fascinated at those parts of the machines from which the finished products came pouring out. It was the duty of these women to see that these billion mark notes were placed in the right baskets and handed to the officials. They had to keep an eye on every single billion. Officials are so funny sometimes."

George Grosz, who carried his notes around in a knapsack, observed that although many people could not afford even the basic necessities of life during this tragic and confusing period, others seemed to become rich. They were the hoarders.

"Once, at midnight, quite by accident, I met someone who in ordinary life was a cook. In secret, however, he was a magician," Grosz wrote. "We began to discuss the only popular subject of the day: food. Mornings, at breakfast of turnip coffee, mildewed bread and synthetic honey, one discussed lunch. At lunch, of turnip cutlets, muscle pudding and turnip coffee, one discussed a dinner of muscle wurst, gray-green rolls with synthetic honey and cold turnip coffee. Since we were always hungry, our imaginations supplied everything that was lacking.

"In a charming manner of speech, like all magicians, he said that, inasmuch as I was an artist and he liked me, he would help me. He considered that the stupid thing about 'food fantasies' was that they remained unsatisfied."

The cook took Grosz to what seemed to be an uninhabited house, where there were pails of butter, marmalade, Russian caviar, hams and other delicacies piled to the ceiling. "Money has no value anymore . . . so I have been storing things everywhere, even in the corridor," he told the painter. After extracting a promise that he would never mention the treasure trove, he fed his new friend. Grosz kept his word. He did not tell the story until long after the cook had died. But some of his bitterest cartoons show overweight men and women gorging themselves on delicacies, while starving children watch through the window.

Other Germans remember that during those crazy days things became more important than ideas, or work, or honor.

An art dealer in Berlin remembers that, in a strange way, his interest in collecting was fueled by Germany's inflation. "My father was an unsuccessful artist," he said. "He worked in a factory during the day and painted landscapes at night. During the inflation, there wasn't much point in working in the factory, since the paper money the men were paid was worthless. So my father painted all the time. He would turn out twenty or thirty landscapes in one morning, and set up shop at a street corner at noon when the office and factory workers rushed out with their bags of money for a lunch break. He'd probably sold ten pictures before in his whole life, mostly to relatives. But, in 1923, even a picture of a cow grazing in the sunset painted on canvas was worth more than the picture of a government official printed on cheap paper, which passed for money in those days. So he usually sold out everything he had worked on during the morning. Then he'd rush to the nearest food store, buy what little food was available, and then rush to the post office to buy the latest editions of million, billion and trillion mark stamps. He was convinced that some of these stamps would be valuable some day, since so few were printed at one time. After all, a 1 million mark stamp printed today would not be enough to mail a postcard tomorrow. My father never put those stamps on letters. He put them away in a bureau drawer. Sure enough, several years after the inflation was over (and my father was back in the factory, selling an occasional painting to a great-aunt), those stamps had indeed become valuable. They helped put me through the university."

He points out that, perhaps subconsciously, he became convinced that collecting things might be more profitable than making things. "A psychiatrist once told me that that's why I'm a succesful art dealer," he said.

However, the incredible situation had a more profound effect on a great many Germans. Blue-collar workers and middle-class families lost faith in many of the virtues they had prized. What good was thrift, if a man's lifetime savings could be wiped out overnight? What good was honesty, if the honest worker starved while the dishonest hoarder (Grosz's "magician") prospered? How could anyone trust a government that allowed these terrible events to happen? What good was democracy when it provided neither security, nor stability, nor hope?

None of the men and women who told of their experiences in the last years of the German democracy and the first years of the Nazi era can remember, from personal experience, the weeks and months of the great inflation. It happened before most of them were born. But not one of those interviewed failed to mention it as a cause for the failure of Germany's democratic experiment. The inflation ended almost as suddenly as it began, but it had shaken many families completely. When Hitler came to power, many of those who told their stories mentioned that their parents said: "Well, I certainly don't agree with everything that that man says . . . but he won't allow that kind of inflation to happen, ever again."

At the height of the German inflation, people would stand in line at slaughterhouses to buy meat as soon as it became available. If they waited for the meat to reach the butcher store, beef or pork might have gone from 6 million marks a pound to 12 million marks a pound within hours.   COURTESY ULLSTEIN BILDERDIENST

Artist Käthe Kollwitz was a painter who conveyed, through her work, the sense of despair that gripped Germany in the late 1920s and early 30s, that contributed to the feeling that "nothing could get worse" and that Hitler might actually represent an improvement over present suffering. Her work, too was banned by the Nazis.

PHOTOGRAPH BY SHARON MATTHEWS

Cartoonist George Grosz had an almost infallible eye for the smugness and hypocrisy that characterized some members of the German middle and upper classes, who helped Hitler come to power. His drawings and paintings were, of course, banned and he was forced to flee his country when Hitler became chancellor. DRAWING: Three Figures in a Bar.

A page from George Grosz's sketchbook, showing typical Berlin types. Many experts have speculated that Hitler, an ordinary, unimposing little man, fascinated so many Germans because he seemed so much like them. The man at the bottom right of the sketch looks like thousands of Germans ... and very much like Hitler, whom Grosz had never met.   PHOTOGRAPH BY SHARON MATTHEWS

A drawing, made by Hitler during his twenties, when he still harbored ambitions of becoming one of the world's great architects. There are those who regret that the university admissions committee couldn't have had prophetic visions of the future: one more bad architect would have done little harm. Once Hitler turned political leader, it changed the fate of the whole world.

Hitler's facial expression could change in seconds, from kind and fatherly to furious and vengeful. He used his acting ability well, especially in speeches, which might start on a note of sweet reason and end in waves of hysterical hatred. Usually he carried his audiences along with his own moods. COURTESY NATIONAL ARCHIVES

Street fights were part of Hitler's strategy in the early 1930s, before he came to power. The more blood was spilled, the more people would wish for law and order at the expense of freedom and justice, he calculated. He was right. Here a brown-shirted street fighter has fallen in one of the brawls that became almost daily events in Germany's cities.

Groups of young men were always featured at party rallies. They enjoyed the rallies, and it gave them a sense of participation in their country, which many remember sadly to this day.

Girls as well as boys joined the Hitler Youth. Most remember the early days of camping, singing and backpacking as some of the most fun-filled in their lives. Few understood how unquestioning obedience and political education were carefully included in those hiking trips and songfests.

COURTESY NATIONAL ARCHIVES

Germans watch in horror as the German Reichstag, the parliament of the Republic, burns in 1933. It had been constructed with special, supposedly fireproof features, and the intensity and the speed of the flames made it clear that the fire had been set deliberately by someone who was an expert in arson.   COURTESY ULLSTEIN BILDERDIENST

The German Reichstag was a hollow shell after the fire, which Hitler accused "the Communists" of setting, and which gave him the excuse he needed to declare martial law. Martial law was never lifted, and later documents revealed that the fire had probably been set deliberately by his henchmen.   COURTESY GERMAN INFORMATION CENTER

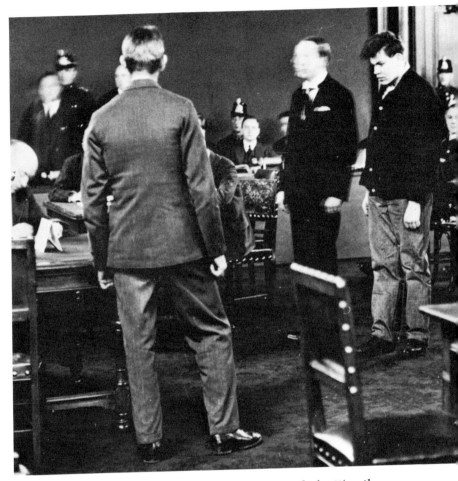

Several so-called Communists and radicals were accused of setting the Reichstag fire at a show trial in 1933. By then, Hitler had not yet succeeded in totally corrupting the court system, and several of the defendants, who had good lawyers and could prove conclusively that they had been nowhere near the building, were acquitted. One defendant, a retarded young man named Marinus van der Lubbe, who did not have the means of obtaining an adequate defense, was convicted and beheaded. After the war it became clear that he, too, had been innocent. Eventually, the courts became corrupted, the judges feared for their own lives, and no one whom the Nazis wished convicted was ever acquitted in a trial receiving national publicity. COURTESY NATIONAL ARCHIVES

The enthusiasm that many young Germans felt for their new leader was genuine. It was compounded of hope for a better, juster future, a pride in the revival of their country, and an instinctive feeling that, somehow, Hitler was more than a political figure . . . he was, in and of himself, a new Germany.

In the early Hitler years, the sight of thousands of uniformed men marching through the streets gave many Germans a feeling of pride. Germany had been disarmed by the Versailles treaty after World War I . . . and soldiers to them represented a new, strong, proud country.

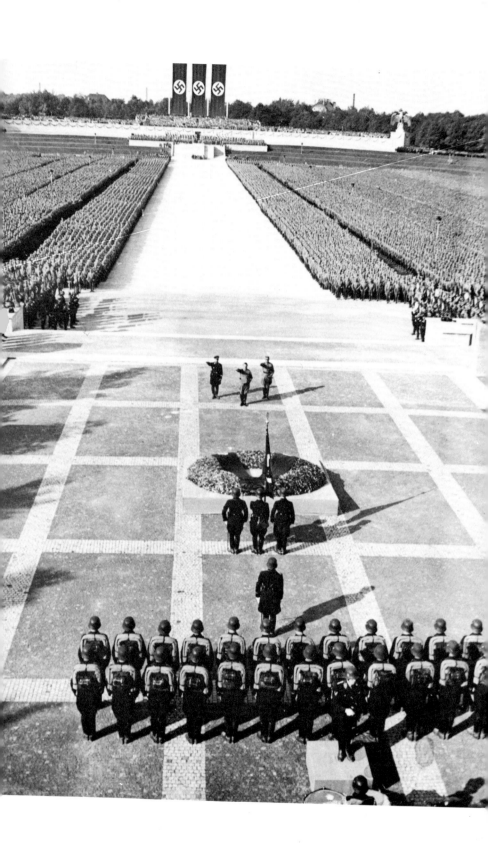

Once a year, at the Nuremberg Party Assembly, Hitler and his top aides celebrated their ascension to power. Almost all the men whose faces can be recognized are now dead . . . many executed for war crimes after the Nuremberg trials.

Hitler, in his early years, had often repeated Emperor Nero's prescription for a contented population that would not revolt against unreasonable rule: "Bread and Circuses." The annual party festivals at Nuremberg were the most spectacular "circuses" Germany had ever seen. Even those who couldn't go could participate, watching films in party halls, motion picture theaters and other gathering places. Usually the audience cheered itself hoarse.

GERMANY IN THE 1930s: "HATE EXPLODED SUDDENLY"

"Hate exploded suddenly, without warning, out of nowhere, at street corners, in restaurants, cinemas, dance halls, swimming baths, at midnight, after breakfast, in the middle of the afternoon . . ."

—*Christopher Isherwood in* THE BERLIN STORIES, *a novel on which the motion picture* CABARET *was based.*

"You didn't have to see any street fighting to know that things were going wrong. People *knew* that there was a sort of Hitler underground, that kids were being indoctrinated, that democratic teachers were getting fired, that the Nazis were better organized than the newspapers ever told us. And there was a quality of political anger. Fierce arguments. We're beginning to have it in New York. If a foreigner were to come here now and just watch our television . . . I know we're not having a revolution here now . . . or are we? You laugh . . . see, that's the way it was then, just the way we are sitting here now. We laughed at the danger. And we didn't *have* any television. But I *heard* about this meeting, that riot, somebody disappearing, I couldn't wait to get away. And I had been in love with Berlin."

—*Pianist, Abram Chasins, as quoted in* BEFORE THE DELUGE *by Otto Friedrich.*

Of course, hate didn't really explode suddenly in 1930. Hate for Jews, for "traitors," for the liberal press (which as the bearer of bad news was often regarded as the cause of all the disasters), and for politicians who seemed to promise a better life but couldn't deliver even a few more jobs, had been smoldering in Germany ever since the end of World War I. Inflation had helped. But there were other problems, too.

And some drastic changes really began in 1930. There had been some unemployment throughout the 1920s, but by 1930 what had been a bothersome problem turned into an acute disaster. In just one month, January, the number of unemployed soared from 1.5 million to almost 2.5 million. From then on, the figures kept climbing steadily. People who had always considered their jobs completely secure suddenly found themselves standing in the long lines that stretched outside of government employment offices, waiting for the stamp that would give them their so-called unemployment insurance, amounting to about $17.50 per month for a family—regardless of the size of the family.

Those who still had jobs were forced to take pay cuts. If they refused, there were thousands of others willing to climb over bodies to get at that precious available job.

Farmers could no longer sell crops, although people in Germany were starving. Students graduated from college into a world that had no place for them. After working hard to get into the university and then spending many years cramming for tough, ever-recurring competitive examinations, many of these students felt betrayed by their country, as did the thousands of shopkeepers whose businesses failed. Men left wives and families they could no longer support, and desperate women took to the streets. The one business that flourished in those seemingly hopeless weeks and months were the pawnshops. Germans had always regarded a pawnshop as the last resort of the drunk or worthless weakling. Now respectable middle-class men and women (especially women) could be seen sneaking into the back door of many a newly opened pawnshop, carrying a precious piece of family silver under a coat or shawl.

Young people going to school in those days often had to pass through crowds of unemployed men and women, many not much older than they, and they naturally wondered: "Is this going to happen to me in a few years?"

Bitter, defeated men gathered at bars and beer halls, trying to pinpoint the cause for Germany's economic disaster. Few realized that the whole world, America included, was going through a depression. They thought that their country had been singled out for misery by "those foreigners," who were, of course, becoming rich through Germany's poverty.

Although only the leader of a small right-wing political movement, Hitler and one of his most brilliant associates, Joseph Goebbels (who would become the first official "Minister of Propaganda" the world had ever known a few years later), naturally saw these beer halls and bars as recruiting grounds for potential followers. The time was ripe for their message, for the Nazi party to begin a move forward.

By reinforcing all the prejudices of the men whom life had apparently failed, telling them that their inability to find work, to lead a decent life, to support their families, was a planned plot by their old enemies, the liberals, the Jews and the scheming politicians, the Nazi party added thousands of new, fighting-mad members to its ranks every month.

Another recruiting area for the Nazis were the tent cities that arose in the forests surrounding Berlin and other tough urban areas. Many of the unemployed had lost their small homes or been evicted from their apartments and they gathered in these cities to seek shelter from the rain and cold. One of these cities was near a lake we sometimes visited on weekends. "Why are these people camping out in the middle of the winter?" a friend asked, as we passed by a tent city, with streets neatly laid out and women cooking turnip soup over camp fires. "They have nowhere else to go," someone answered.

Every Saturday and Sunday brown-shirted men, Nazis, in longer and longer columns, marched through the streets of Berlin and Munich. By the end of the year they were marching through the suburbs. They often sang a song which began: *"The flag held high, our rows of comrades closed . . ."* The song had been written by a man called Horst Wessel, a dedicated Nazi who in private life was a criminal, making his living on organized prostitution and drugs. He was shot by a fellow mobster in a fight over a woman. As he lay dying in a hospital, Goebbels visited him constantly. In their newspapers, the Nazi party issued daily bulletins on his condition.

It seemed that the attacker, Ali Hohler, might have once belonged to a Communist street gang. The attack was interpreted by Goebbels as political—another reactionary blow at a fine and honest comrade. When Wessel died, there was a tremendous funeral, with thousands of brown-shirted men marching behind the coffin, singing Wessel's song, which became the official anthem of the Nazi party. The flag these men carried was not the black, red and gold striped symbol of the German Republic, but a new one, in the old colors of the German Empire—black, red and white. However, instead of stripes, it had a red background and a white circle, containing a black symbol that to many of us was still unfamiliar: the swastika. Actually, the German word for swastika is much more descriptive: *Hakenkreuz*, a cross with hooks.

In those days, Communists and Socialists also marched—although not in the suburbs, or even, very often, in the center of the cities. In Berlin they concentrated their efforts in such poverty ghettos as Neukoeln. And, although few people ever saw police attack a column of brown-shirted Hitler followers (they seemed orderly enough, after all, at least during the daytime hours, in full view of their audiences), the marchers in Neukoeln were frequently disbursed by police. Often the police carried nightsticks and later, guns. The marchers were rarely armed with anything but pamphlets and slogans.

The street fighting reflected some of the confusion within

the government. The country, at the beginning of 1930, was ruled by a coalition government, which had elected a chancellor, Hermann Mueller. The president of Germany was that eternal old man, General von Hindenburg, who had presided so hesitantly at the birth of Germany's shaky democracy, and who, by now, was almost senile. However, since the office of president was supposed to be largely a ceremonial one, with the chancellor carrying much of the executive responsibility, nobody seriously thought of replacing Hindenburg.

Mueller was a very sick man. He had suffered from a serious liver ailment for years, and when he was told that Hindenburg would really prefer a new and stronger man as chancellor, he resigned. According to many historians, that resignation marked the end of true parliamentary government in Germany until after World War II.

Mueller died about a year later, and his funeral was one of the last great state occasions at which the red, black and gold flag was flown.

With Mueller's resignation, the executive powers of the government passed into the hands of Hindenburg, who was eighty-three years old and, according to the best evidence from his associates of those years, probably could not have served competently as the mayor of a town with a population of 1,000. He had lapses of memory, often did not recognize people he had known for years, and apparently left the running of the country to a small group of corrupt men, elected by no one, who flattered him and pretended to carry out his every wish.

The next chancellor was picked by this group. He was a totally honest man: Dr. Heinrich Bruening, the leader of the Center party, which controlled about one-fifth of the Reichstag. There was little hope that he would ever be able to rally a majority to his side, but the men around Hindenburg apparently wanted a weak chancellor so that they could unofficially rule the country themselves. In many ways Bruening surprised them. He tried to bring some order into the economic and social chaos he found around him. Since the country's treasury, as well as many of its people, was threatened by bankruptcy, he ordered a cut in the unemployment insurance and cuts in the pay of government workers. Many industries followed suit: those that had already cut workers' pay, cut it further; and those who had not yet succumbed to the general trend, instituted lower salaries. These moves obviously didn't make Bruening popular. He became known as, "the Chancellor of Hunger." What's more, even the Reichstag rejected his austerity program. So Bruening used the weapon that had been built into the German Constitution from the beginning: Article 48, authorizing him to rule by decree in an emergency.

The austerity program would be put into effect, whether the Reichstag approved or not. Other orders were given in an attempt to stem the chaos in the streets. Marches and outdoor meetings were prohibited by the Prussian State government. (Since most of the physical violence took place in Berlin, it didn't seem necessary to issue a national decree.) When Nazi uniforms and flags were also banned, the Nazis simply switched from brown to white shirts, covering their shirt buttons with the caps of beer bottles, so that everybody would know who they were. They marched less and organized more.

Few, except insiders, knew that at this time a bitter struggle was going on inside the Nazi party itself. The real name for the party had always been the National Socialist Party. Hitler emphasized the "national" aspects of his ideas and left plans for political reform deliberately vague, but there were others around him who took that term "socialist" very seriously. They talked in very specific terms about the nationalization of German industry and the breaking up of some of the huge land-holdings of the superrich former German aristocracy.

At the same time, many of these wealthy industrialists and landholders had long seen Hitler as their savior from Communism. Contributions to his party had come in, not only from German industry, but from industrialists in other countries who also saw the Nazi party as a dam against the Communist or Socialist flood that was threatening to engulf Europe. Hitler himself received money from a personal trust fund, set up by some of these men so that he could live in the style they felt became a political leader. So did Hermann Goering, the former air-force ace, who was used to attract "respectable" former soldiers and patriots, who for a time had regarded Hitler as uncouth and socially unacceptable.

Hitler considered himself a Socialist, but hated Marxism. It's doubtful to many of those who had studied his life and ideas that he understood the difference. He *did* know that Karl Marx had been a Jew, and no Jewish ideology could possibly be acceptable in a racially pure Germany. Some of those present at a meeting where the question of "socialism" was finally thrashed out reported later that Hitler simply announced he was a Socialist. After all, he was an ordinary working man. But there was to be no more Marxist ideology. "What you preach is liberalism . . . just liberalism," he accused some of the more ardent Socialist radicals in his party. He often emphasized that what the average, middle-class German wanted was "bread and circuses," not soft-headed idealism or bleeding heart social theory. "We can never hope to win the workers by an appeal to ideas," he said in many of his early speeches. "That's been tried, and it just didn't get our opponents anywhere, and it won't help us either. The workers want revolution . . . and that's what we'll give them."

When several of the party comrades objected, he had them beaten up by loyal followers. He also had a long memory. Some of those who had opposed him on the Socialist issue early, and who might well have forgotten their disputes with their leader, were murdered in a bloodletting of the Nazi party in 1936. Also murdered, incidentally, was the obscure minor mobster who had killed Horst Wessel. After the Nazis came to power they went to the prison where Hohler had been sent (he was sentenced to life imprisonment), took him into the woods and killed him.

By the summer of 1930, the Nazi party was in fighting trim

—its internal struggles apparently solved, its numbers growing with every passing month, and Hitler, who only a few years before had been an obscure, ridiculed man, was a political power to be taken seriously.

Bruening, meanwhile, had dissolved the Reichstag, which had refused to approve his austerity program. In spite of advice from almost all of his associates, he felt that an election had to be called, no later than September of 1930. The election took place on September 14, 1930. Until then very few politicians and almost no political analysts or journalists had apparently understood how strong the Nazi party had become.

On reading over German papers for the months of June, July and August, it becomes obvious that the vast majority of political reporters, columnists and editors still considered Hitler and his band of conspicuous followers a very minor menace. There were about thirty daily papers in Berlin, and only those that were specifically oriented toward the Nazi party predicted any significant gains in Hitler's parliamentary delegation. All agreed that the party had grown stronger. After all, it had held only 12 seats in the Reichstag, and the Brownshirts in the Berlin streets certainly showed that there was a potential for more than that. Some of the most informed journalists (including those in the liberal press that Hitler despised) predicted that the Nazis might hold as many as 50 or 60 seats. Actually the party had 107, making it the second strongest party in Germany. The number of people voting for the party rose from 810,000 (who might well be dismissed as the lunatic right-wing fringe that appears in every country) to 6.5 million.

It was obvious to many Germans as the election results were announced over the radio that something basic had changed. Since the beginning of the Weimar Republic, Germany had gone through many chancellors; majorities in the Reichstag had shifted; new parties had been established, risen and then vanished. Because there were so many splinter parties (Germany, like France, and unlike Great Britain and the United

States, had never had a strong two- or three-party system, sometimes there were as many as twenty parties), peaceful compromises always seemed possible.

Even after the 1930 election, the Social Democrats, who had been the largest party and who, in coalition with many of the splinter parties, had been in control of the country from the beginning of Germany's accidental democracy, still had the most seats: 143, 36 more than Hitler's National Socialists. The Communists, whose influence also had risen somewhat, had 77. The total was 577 seats. However, the coalitions and reasonable accomodations that had been made to hold crumbling governments together in the past were impossible once the Nazis held so much power. Almost all those who really understood German politics knew this would be true from the start. Another musician, cellist Emanuel Feuermann, who listened to the news of those 6.5 million votes on the radio, was quoted again by author Otto Friedrich, as saying sadly: "It's all over with Germany, all over with Europe."

Then he left the room. Shortly thereafter he left Germany; and a great many other artists, writers, scientists, political leaders, journalists and other intellectuals slowly began an exodus, which climaxed in 1933 when Hitler took over the country completely. Between 1930 and 1933 there were a number of chancellors, but none of them were able to give the country a stable government. Finally, in January of 1933, Hitler demanded to be made chancellor. He was, and democracy was dead in Germany.

HITLER

"At the time of the reoccupation of the Rhineland in 1936, Hitler made use of an extraordinary figure of speech in describing his own conduct. He said: 'I follow my course with the precision and security of a sleepwalker.'"

—*William C. Langer, psychoanalyst,*
in THE MIND OF ADOLF HITLER.

". . . his appearance also surprised me. On posters and in caricatures I had seen him in military tunic, with shoulder straps, swastika armband, and hair flapping on his forehead. But here he was wearing a well-fitted blue suit and looking markedly respectable. Everything about him bore out a note of reasonable modesty. Later I learned that he had a great gift for adjusting—consciously or intuitively—to his surroundings."

—*Albert Speer, on his first encounter with*
Adolf Hitler at a university meeting, from his
autobiography, INSIDE THE THIRD REICH.

"Ask the Commandant whether he's ever met Hitler in person," said Joan, whose German was somewhat sloppy.

The Commandant turned toward her: "Yes, I indeed have

talked with my Führer face-to-face," he answered slowly in English, then lapsed again into German: "For only five minutes, and yet he is so transparent I feel I have known him the whole of my life. I shall tell you exactly about him. He's . . . well, to begin with he's what a Christian would call a 'saint' . . . there's no other word for the manifest supernatural power working through him; and yet he's as simple and unassuming to meet as you and me. And gentle: all children love him at sight. But he has one fault: so pure and honest himself he's a little gullible—easily hoodwinked by self-seeking rascals hanging on to his coat-tails. But then, he's a man so loyal to all his friends that he won't hear a word against them . . . more's the pity in certain cases . . ."

—*Richard Hughes, from the novel* THE WOODEN SHEPHERDESS,
*in which a well-meaning and thoroughly
converted Youth Corps leader
describes his reaction to Hitler.*

These three descriptions of Adolf Hitler, two by men who never met him (the psychiatrist and the novelist) and the other by one of his intimate associates (Albert Speer), have one factor in common: they make him seem relatively harmless. This is no accident. Hitler attempted to be all things to all men. To a group of students he could appear as a moderate, rather mild politician. In public he preferred to be seen as a gentle man, who loved children and cared so much for animals that he became a vegetarian. His speeches were often so irrational that politicians flatly refused to take him seriously. After all, who among his domestic and foreign adversaries would be afraid of a man who publicly announced that he was "following a course with the precision and security of a sleepwalker?"

He deliberately kept himself shrouded in mystery. For a long time historians accepted his own accounts of his childhood and youth. Little of what he told about himself turned out to be true. He was a master image builder and did not hesitate to alter his own personal history to fit the picture he knew the German people would prefer to the simple facts. He told of a poverty-stricken childhood and youth, in a family so beset by adversity that it was continually on the ragged edge of starvation, of a father who was denied employment and advancement by his enemies, of a mother who was forced to work herself almost to death, of discrimination against him (because of his background and ideas) in schooling and employment.

What are the real facts? We know that Hitler was born on April 20, 1889, in the small Austrian border town of Branau-Am-Inn and that the family moved later to a slightly larger town. We know he had three brothers and two sisters. One brother died, not of poverty and hunger as Hitler would occasionally indicate in one of his more self-pitying speeches, but of measles. His father was an out-of-wedlock child, and sometimes used the name "Schickelgruber," which had been his mother's maiden name, rather than "Hitler," which was the name of the man she never married. Young Adolf realized very early that Adolf Schickelgruber somehow lacked the heroic ring that he felt he needed. He never used the name. Far from living in abysmal poverty, the family was rather well off. His father had a secure income, a savings account, and owned his own home. After he retired, he received a generous pension.

As a child, Hitler did exceedingly badly in school. This accounted for his inability to go to a pre-university school, called a *Gymnasium*, rather than a *Realschule*, which has less prestige and prepares its graduates for technical and commercial careers. Throughout his life Hitler blamed his family's poverty for his lack of educational opportunity. Obviously, the facts were quite different. He barely made it even through the commercial high school.

He was unpopular with classmates and spent a great deal of time alone. He read little except the novels of a German writer of trash fiction who wrote about the American West in highly romantic and racist terms.

This writer, Karl May, was exceedingly popular with almost all German children (including myself). Without ever leaving Germany, he wrote about an American cowboy, "Old Shatterhand," and his desperate struggle with a tribe of Indians, "the Oglala." A sort of Lone Ranger with vicious overtones, Old Shatterhand rode about with his loyal Indian companion, the noble Winnetou, by his side, slaughtering whole bands of nasty, cunning, immoral redskins. When May got tired of the old West, he transferred Shatterhand to the Middle East, where he proceeded to slaughter bands of the local natives, dark-skinned members of nasty, cunning, immoral Arab tribes. The novels were full of action and violence, and when we were between the ages of ten and twelve, we admired them extravagantly. However, most of us outgrew our admiration for Karl May by the time we hit our thirteenth birthday, and laughed at his simplistic philosophy and his ridiculous historical and geographic inaccuracies. Hitler never did. He continued reading Karl May well into adulthood. "I owe Karl May my first idea of geography," he was quoted later as saying, "and, in fact, he opened my eyes to the world." The lessons in inaccurate geography were probably fairly harmless. The constant exposure to a world of violence, hatred, bloodshed and racism apparently were not, since they fit so well into the fantasy world that Hitler was beginning to create for himself.

Hitler's father died in 1903 and left the family a pension, a bank account and a house. In 1905 his mother sold the house, not because she was forced to do so for financial reasons (Hitler sometimes darkly hinted that the "Jewish moneylenders" were behind the sale), but because she wished to live in a larger town.

By that time Hitler had graduated from school and was planning a career as an artist. His mother seems to have supported his ambition, since she apparently never complained about her son who stayed in his room most of the day, refused to look for work, and only tentatively tried to gain admission to art school. She provided an allowance and room and board. When she died in 1907, Hitler was on his own, although he still had a small pension from his father's estate. He moved to Vienna, applied at the Academy of Fine Arts, and was turned down. Anyone who has ever seen his drawings and architectural sketches does not have to look any further for an explanation of the academy's refusal to admit him. He was a bad artist. Hitler, however, used his by now familiar rationalization for his failure: the art world was dominated by Jews and other undesirables, and they were afraid that he would become a world-famous painter, so of course they had to keep him down.

By now he was really poor. He drifted from boardinghouse to boardinghouse, supplementing his small income by drawing picture postcards. Once he visited his brother, who had moved to England. It is evident from letters written by the brother and his wife that they couldn't wait to get rid of their uninvited houseguest.

In 1913 Hitler moved to Munich to avoid service in the Austrian army. However, when World War I broke out, he volunteered for the German army and served with some distinction throughout the war years. His letters indicate that he rather enjoyed the war. At least he wasn't lonely anymore. He was awarded a medal (at the recommendation of his Jewish first lieutenant—a fact that he tried to keep hidden for the rest of his life), and in October of 1918, when the war was almost over, was overcome by chlorine gas in a French infantry attack. Two days later he was in an army hospital, totally blind. Most psychiatrists today, examining that episode of blindness, call it a "hysterical reaction," i.e., there was almost nothing the matter with his eyes and a great deal wrong with his emotions. The war ended on November 11, and Hitler experienced an attack of blind fury combined with panic, a reaction undoubtedly shared by many of his fellow-Germans. Several of his biographers assume that at this low point in his own life and that of his country, he decided that Germany needed a savior and he was to be the chosen one.

Based on his previous record, one might have thought that his chances of being elected even to a minor village post would be small. Here was a man who couldn't get along with anyone in his family except his mother, who couldn't make or keep friends, who had been a failure in school and in his chosen profession. He was penniless and physically unattractive. In short, he had none of the qualities one might imagine would be needed for even a minor career in politics. But Hitler never thought in terms of politics. He hated and despised professional politicians. He thought of government in terms of power, absolute rule, and sacrifice and obedience to a single leader.

In a strange way his attitudes and even his failures fitted into a rather special German romantic tradition. The heroes Hitler and most other German children had been taught to look up to were always loners, pitted by fate against an evil society. They were filled with stormy emotions and given to shouting and shaking of fists (or swords). Frequently they lost their lives to the forces of evil, and were then avenged by new lonely, remote figures, who wiped out the evil forces and stood, triumphant, surrounded by the corpses of their enemies. Unlike the knights of King Arthur's Round Table, these heroes never sought for peace or justice; their only distinction was a determination to fight their foes to the death. Neither was there ever any clear definition of the "evil" those marvelous heroes were destroying. The myths were not that explicit.

Not only German mythology, but German literature as well, was full of lonely, misunderstood young men, yearning for strife and sacrifice, full of violence and anger. The German king most schoolchildren had been taught to admire was Frederick of Prussia (referred to in Germany as "Frederick the Great") who, after a stormy childhood and youth (with his father as one of his most punishing enemies), rose to win wars to enhance the greatness of Germany. Hitler patterned himself after Frederick the Great, although he affected to despise German aristocracy as much as professional politicians.

Hitler, in a strange way, was able to use his liabilities and turn them into assets that fitted well into a set of German fantasies. He had failed in his youth because, according to him, a powerful, evil conspiracy had blocked him at every turn. He could not show love to his family or a friend, or even a woman, because he was so filled with an overwhelming love of the whole German people that no energy was left for any personal relationships. He looked ordinary enough, but large numbers of other ordinary-looking people were able to identify with him; and once they had accepted him as their leader, they were able to forget that he was really a rather short man with poor skin, narrow shoulders and a shock of often dirty hair on his forehead. They would talk about his mystical eyes (nobody ever seemed to remember the color, which was described as everything from violet to black, but was actually a rather greenish blue), which according to popular legend penetrated right to a man's soul and could spot evil that ordinary mortals could not perceive. For many, Hitler became a symbol of all they themselves wanted to be: powerful, great, and able to command events rather than be commanded by them. In 1919, with a tiny following of fanatical supporters, he started on his way. By 1933—still appearing to an objective observer to be an irrational, spiteful, rather unintelligent and uneducated little man—he had become one of the most powerful rulers in history. A lost war, a disastrous inflation, disorder and crime, and many lost German illusions had helped to put him in power. But so had some other rather special German problems: an educational system that emphasized obedience over independent thought; a series of orators who taught the public to distrust a free press; an overwhelming longing for order and stability, even at the expense of freedom and justice.

It seems inconceivable to most people who did not live through the early Hitler years that one such man could have gained such complete and disastrous control of a country without the majority of its citizens rebelling. But freedom, in Germany, seeped away, rather than disappearing overnight. When Hitler took over the government in 1933, it was not apparent to most people that he had either the wish or the power to overthrow the German democracy. He certainly had expressed his contempt for it frequently enough in his book (which hardly anybody had read) and in his speeches (which too few took seriously). But most Germans believed that something or somebody would protect them from total disaster. After all, their constitution had not been repealed. There were the labor unions, the industrialists and the military, some of whom supported Hitler up to a point, but who surely would not allow him to take over total power.

Hitler destroyed the unions immediately. He won many of the most powerful industrialists over to his side, and then destroyed them, too, when it suited his purposes. The military leadership recognized too late that it too had lost all power. When, in the summer of 1944, some of the generals finally realized that they were incapable of stopping Germany's headlong race to disaster, they even plotted to kill Hitler. But the military establishment, like other sectors of German life, was thoroughly infiltrated with spies. The plot failed. The rebelling generals were executed: many of them were strangled on meat hooks after horrible tortures. How could one man so completely change not only the history of his country, but that of the whole world?

The average German, whose life in the early years was not much affected by political changes, probably hardly noticed the creeping dictatorship. Later, most Germans were proud of Hitler's international triumphs. Chairman Mao struck a deep psychological note that applies, apparently, to citizens of almost any country, when he remarked that power grows from the barrel of a gun. Most Germans, certainly, believed that they had been dishonorably disarmed by the Versailles treaty, and that no weapons meant no power. That Hitler could rearm Germany, reoccupy the Rhineland and take over German-speaking Austria with no more than a weak protest from the most powerful nations on earth, gave them a sense of pride and accomplishment.

Hitler's invasions of other countries at the beginning of World War II were instantly successful, and most Germans triumphed in their country's triumph. As one liberal member of the present Reichstag put it: "Of course I joined the army. Everybody did. It was considered one's patriotic duty . . . and few of us had any second thoughts about Germany's actions until we started to lose the war, and our own cities were bombed and our own lands invaded."

Many Germans who are now middle-aged and who remember the Hitler years talk about these special problems to explain what happened in their country. In looking at their stories, their explanations seem the most logical ones.

THINKING BACK

"First there's the children's house of make-believe,
Some shattered dishes underneath a pine,
The playthings in the playhouse of children.
Weep for what little things could make them glad.
Then for the house that is no more a house,
But only a belilaced cellar hole,
Now slowly closing like a dent in dough.
This was no playhouse but a house in earnest . . ."

Robert Frost.

Not until about 1930 did most German adults even become aware of Adolf Hitler and his movement as a political presence, threatening or promising, depending on their point of view. Most German teenagers apparently were very little concerned with politics. Now, as adults, they may remember vague political discussions in their parents' homes. But almost none can recall a single instance of political discussion at school. Even if they joined supposedly political groups, they usually did so for nonpolitical reasons.

"We were taught history as a series of facts," said Klaus, whose entire life changed because his mother was Jewish. "We had to learn dates, names, places of battles. Periods during which Germany won wars were emphasized. Periods during which Germany lost wars were sloughed over. We heard very little about World War I, except that the Versailles peace treaty was a disgrace, which someday, in some vague way, would be rectified. In my school, one of the best in Berlin, there were three courses in Greek and Roman history, four in medieval history, and not one in government. If we tried to relate ideas we got from literature or history to current events, our teachers changed the subject.

"I really don't believe that anyone was deliberately trying to evade politics. Those teachers really seemed to think that what went on in the Greek and Roman Empire was more important than what was happening on the streets of Berlin and Munich. They considered any attempt to bring up current political questions a distraction . . . we were probably trying to talk about something that didn't concern the course because we hadn't done our homework.

"And there was always a great deal of homework in a school like mine, which prepared students for the university. At the end· of our senior year, we were expected to take a detailed and exceedingly tough exam called the *Abitur*. How we did on this exam could determine our whole future. Again, the *Abitur* concentrated on our knowledge of *facts*, not on interpretation or on the expression of personal ideas. Looking back on it now, it also didn't seem to measure our ability to reason clearly . . . to draw conclusions, to interpret ideas. However, we were expected to take both Latin and Greek in our last years of school, plus a great deal of German literature and history, natural science, mathematics, and at least one modern language. Most of us took French, because English somehow was considered utilitarian, while French was elegant.

"Looking back now, I feel that we were being prepared for nothing except to be hardworking, uninvolved university students. Certainly with the kind of education we got, none of us was ready to take a job. Also, we were not regarded as citizens . . . we were looked upon as children, up to the age of twenty-five."

But in spite of all this hard work, Klaus remembers the years between 1930 and 1933 as the happiest of his life. "I had some problems at home," he says. "My parents, especially my mother, were very ambitious for me. I was the only child, and was expected to become a professor or a physician. They kept after me constantly to make sure that my grades were high and that I was getting ready for that all important *Abitur*. In my senior year I took seven major subjects, and often worked until midnight. However, most of my friends were in the same spot . . . *their* parents were giving them a hard time, too. Looking at today's teenagers in Germany, it's amazing to me that some of us didn't rebel more . . . but we didn't. We had been taught carefully that talking back to people in authority was more than bad manners . . . it was plain, outright immorality and a sign of a bad character besides."

Klaus loved music and the theater, and there were a great many good plays and concerts in Berlin. He went on his student pass on Saturdays, and saw and heard many of the outstanding artists of that time, men and women who three or four years later would leave Germany for England or the United States, because they were no longer welcome in their own country. "Many of the plays I saw were very political," he said. "But again, although I was fascinated by the ideas, I never translated them from the stage into real life. If the working class was fighting for survival in a play by Bertold Brecht, that was *theater* . . . it wasn't even remotely related to the street fights between strikers and policemen I sometimes observed on my way to school. That was one of the worst features of the way most of us were educated . . . we simply were unable to draw conclusions. Or perhaps our teachers and our parents deliberately tried to protect us from real life, either because they thought of us as children, or because they were already vaguely frightened about the future and didn't want to become involved themselves."

Klaus was not interested in sports, but many of his friends were. And there were innumerable opportunities to play soccer, swim, go on hikes, bicycle or work out in well-equipped gyms, available almost free-of-charge. Anyone showing any talent in a sport was encouraged and given every chance to improve his skills, as a member of a school team or a youth club. But even there, group activity was approved, individual action was not. "I liked to wander in the woods around Berlin," Klaus said. "So my mother enrolled me in a hiking club. I pointed out tactfully that this was not what I had in mind. Marching around the countryside, singing sentimental German folk songs with twenty other boys, was not my idea of fun. I liked to stroll around by myself . . . enjoying the quiet and the scenery. My mother somehow gave me to understand that this was unmasculine . . . and what's more, un-German.

"There was a great deal of control over my life and that of my friends . . . from the school and from parents. But somehow we all felt that this was necessary, so that we could get through that *Abitur*, get into a good university . . . and be free," Klaus said. "We lived for the future. We had to think very little, take almost no initiative, our days were charted out for us. It seems strange that with bloody street fights almost every weekend, groups of brown-shirted men singing aggressive songs on Saturday morning as they marched to their training grounds, political assassinations on the front pages of the papers regularly, we never felt threatened, never afraid of anything but failure in school. Perhaps our parents were more aware of what was happening, but I don't think so. Usually parents aren't all that good at hiding what they feel from teenage children . . . and I certainly didn't get any impression from mine that they were worried about anything but my father's next raise, the price of meat, whether 'undesirable elements' were moving into the neighborhood (that meant a high-rise apartment house down the block from the town house in which we had lived since I was born) and, of course, my future at the university."

Judging by everything that Klaus said about those parents, they were both intelligent, educated people. And they certainly had more to worry about than many of their neighbors.

Yet the fact that his mother was a Jew, and that anti-Jewish propaganda in Hitler's speeches and in his party newspaper was becoming more vitriolic every month, somehow did not seem to touch them. "My mother considered herself a *German*, not a *Jew*," Klaus said. "She often made snide remarks about the wave of Jewish immigrants that had come to Germany from Poland and Russia to escape persecution there. She considered these people lower class . . . beneath her. She resented the fact that they spoke broken German, often wore beards and long black coats, and deliberately refused to take on the manners and ideas of their adopted country. 'Those people give all Jews a bad name,' she once remarked bitterly, as she watched a group of Yiddish-speaking, foreign-looking men and women come out of a Berlin railroad station."

Klaus did not relate that remark to his own life. He didn't even *know* until after the Nazis came into power that his mother was a Jew, and that therefore, he would be considered a *Mischling* (someone of mixed blood), who would be barred from the university, no matter how high his grades, who would be refused entrance into the theaters and concerts he loved, and who would even be expelled from the hiking club, about which he suddenly started to care when it would no longer accept him. But all of this did not start to happen until three years later.

In many ways, Rosel, growing up in her Bavarian village, remembers the time between 1930 and 1936 an as even happier period than Klaus. There was no pressure on her to perform brilliantly in school. A girl from her background simply did not go to a university, and as long as she kept her grades at passing levels, everybody was happy.

Her relationship with her parents was much warmer than Klaus's was with his family. Her family worked together on the farm with each one assigned his own chores. She had a pet cow, which she milked and took care of, and she was allowed to keep the money from the sale of the milk as an allowance.

The saddest memory of her adolescence was of the time the cow had a calf and it was taken off to the village butcher. "I cried for weeks," she said. "But my parents told me there was no room in the stalls for another animal . . . and anyway, a calf was not a pet . . . it had to be considered as something to increase the family income."

There was another difference between Rosel's family and Klaus's parents. Her father was very active in politics. She knew this because he went to political meetings two evenings a week. Her mother explained that he was a Socialist, that he believed that wealthy factory owners were exploiting German workers, that much of the unemployment that was prevalent in the cities (although not in their village—everybody had a job there) might be avoided if the Government took proper steps, that taxes were unequal, with small farmers, like her parents, paying a great deal too much while owners of huge inherited properties (called *Rittergut*) were paying much too little.

Rosel didn't consider her father's political activity as being in any way threatening to her own life-style. Her best friend's father was an avid soccer player at a soccer club, and she looked upon her father's political club in much the same way as she regarded the soccer club. Some people played soccer, some rowed boats and some went to political meetings. After all, adults had to have some fun too, she thought.

Like Klaus, she learned nothing about German government or politics in school. She didn't take Latin or Greek, and there was no ancient history. Courses concentrated on German history, including two years on the history of Bavaria. She somehow received the impression that Bavarians were quite different from the Prussians who ran things in Berlin, that Bavarians were not respected as much and that one of these days they would have to assert themselves. She tried to discuss these ideas with her parents, who indicated that they agreed with her in a general way but didn't elaborate. When her father told about the work done by his political group, she listened, but she did not relate any of the ideas she heard to her own life, which she considered eminently satisfactory. The stories about unemployment, poverty and despair in the big cities sounded like something out of a book. "It's amazing to me how anyone as naturally curious as I was could have been so innocent and ignorant," she reports now, almost forty years later. "But Germans have always had a very romantic view of childhood . . . at least my parents did. They wanted to protect me from ideas and events that they thought I wouldn't be able to understand or handle. Of course, in a way, that was the worst thing they could have done. When the Nazis came and my father went to prison, when our farm was taken away and my mother died, I was completely unprepared to deal with what had happened. I could not understand why all this terrible misfortune had so suddenly descended on us.

"For a while I thought that perhaps I was responsible in some obscure way, that I had done something terrible, and that God was punishing me through my family. If it had not been for that old history professor, my father's friend, who explained to me that my father was a hero and a martyr and that I should be proud of him, I don't think I could have lived through the frightening years of the late 1930s and early forties. I'll always be grateful for what that old professor did for me . . . but it would have been so much better if my parents had explained to me that my father's political activities were more than a hobby . . . that they reflected a deeply held conviction. Even if he didn't know that he might eventually have to pay for those convictions with his life, I would have been more prepared for what happened had I known something about his ideas and feelings. At any rate, I probably wouldn't have felt that unbearable sense of guilt when the sky seemed to fall in on us. Perhaps I would not have been able to feel proud and free, as the professor suggested I should. I would still have been frightened and sad . . . but at least I would have understood."

Even Hedwig, growing up in her desolate industrial town

in East Prussia, with an unemployed father and a mother who was constantly weary and depressed from overwork and bad nutrition, thought of the years between 1930 and 1936 as a relatively carefree period. The best times she remembers were the months immediately following Hitler's rise to power, when her father, an early Nazi, suddenly had a good job and was considered an important man in the neighborhood in Berlin to which they had moved from the small East Prussian town.

"Before 1933, most of us seemed to be in the same boat," she said. "All my friends' fathers were losing their jobs and living on the edge of poverty. We ate a lot of potatoes and hard black bread with margarine. There was often a Christmas when there were no presents, except perhaps some warm underwear or some new wool stockings. But I had lots of company. My father seemed angry much of the time, and my mother sad. But again, so were the parents of most of my friends. Occasionally, I would go home with a girl in my class at school, and her parents would be very cold to me. This puzzled me, until I found out that in my neighborhood it was known that my father belonged to the Hitler party . . . and that a great many of my friends' fathers were Communists or Socialists. But most of us children considered this a stupid quarrel between adults that didn't concern us.

"We tried to figure out why men who wanted to work didn't get a chance to earn a living. My father would sometimes get drunk and rail at the government and the Jews. He scared me, and I never asked him any questions. My mother, when I brought up the subject, would mutter something about 'God's will.' I left school after the sixth grade and got a job doing housework in a family with four children. My employers seemed kind. They fed me well, and gave me a warm coat to wear in the winter. But when my father, who had never seemed particularly concerned about what I was doing as long as it was not costing him money, found out where I was working, he got furious and made me quit. It turned out that my employers were Jews, and my father told me that they were responsible for all our poverty and unhappiness. I couldn't see that at all.

"After we moved to Berlin, and my father still couldn't get a job, my mother went to work as a maid. My father approved of her employers . . . they were 'racially pure Germans,' he said. But they fed my mother bread and margarine for lunch and made her work until midnight on Christmas Eve. I didn't dare say so, but I thought that my former employers had been much kinder and better.

"My father never tried to interest me in joining in his political activities. I was given to understand that his party comrades didn't think politics was suitable for girls. There just wouldn't be anything for me to do.

"After Hitler came into power and I joined the girls' Hitler Youth Movement, I had a glorious time for a while. But my mother continued to look unhappy and worn. We were Catholics, and she spent more and more time in church. My father was furious at her for not joining the Nazi women's group in the neighborhood. Once, when she came home from Mass, he beat her. He told her in no uncertain terms that the priest in our parish was 'a bad German' because he refused to obey party orders to report members of his congregation with Jewish ancestry to the local authorities. He ordered her to stop associating in any way with the Church. She obeyed . . . and just looked grayer and more unhappy every day. After one party meeting, which he attended in our old hometown as a delegate from Berlin, he told me gloatingly that my former employers had been removed from their home and that their business had been taken over by a 'good Aryan man.' I gathered that meant not a Jew. I admit that this did not bother me very much at the time . . . what did bother me was that some of my friends' fathers, who had been Communists, or Socialists, were arrested and disappeared. While we were living better than ever before, many of these friends were much worse off.

"So the brief time of happiness after Hitler took over didn't last. I remember the years before Hitler as a time when I worried about events that didn't seem to be our fault: lack of work, lack of money, insecurity. Obviously, the fact that my former employer had been expelled from his home and that my friends' fathers kept getting arrested was also not my fault. But I realized, vaguely, that this was what my father had wanted all along, and I now felt guilty. I might add that I have never stopped feeling guilty. So the guilt-free years, even though they were rough, seem like relatively happy ones to me now."

Joachim also remembers the years before Hitler came to full power as exciting, vital and enormously satisfying. He had joined the Hitler Youth almost as soon as the first troop was formed in his neighborhood. Unlike Klaus, Rosel and Hedwig, he thought that he was deeply involved in politics. Actually, he realizes now, that he knew absolutely nothing about the political movement he had so enthusiastically joined and to which he planned to devote his life.

His father had died when he was five. His mother worked as a secretary to a newspaper publisher. He saw her only in the evening, and then she was usually exhausted. Without realizing it, he came to hate the paper that was taking so much of her energy. The paper itself was one of Germany's most respected dailies; published in Frankfurt, it was read by many educated Germans everywhere and served as a source of German news to diplomats and reporters from other countries. The paper's reporting was unusually objective and fair. Many other German papers favored the right or left in the political spectrum and didn't bother to keep their editorial opinions out of their news columns. However, this was not true of the *Frankfurter Algemeine Zeitung*, although its editorial page tended to be on the liberal side. For many reasons, the paper came under special attack regularly in the newspaper published by the Hitler Movement, *Der Voelkischer Beobachter* (which might be translated freely as "The Observer for the People").

Looking back now, Joachim thinks that the started to read the Nazi paper because of his resentment against his mother's job. He also started attending troop meetings of the Hitler Youth Group because he often felt lonely. His mother was appalled when he told her that he had decided to become a member of the group, but he refused to listen to her, and she was too tired to argue.

As part of the movement, he was exposed to many ideas that seemed perfectly logical to him at the time. He was interested in flying, but Germany was not allowed to have an air force. He wanted to build a life based on the legends of the flyers in World War I, especially Baron von Richthofen, the flying ace who had been killed in a dog fight after shooting down a record number of enemy planes, and Hermann Goering, another former flying ace, who was now one of the top leaders in the Nazi party.

As part of his Hitler Youth training, he learned to make model airplanes and was finally made a member of a glider group. He was given to understand that as soon as Hitler came into power, the Versailles treaty would be ignored and Germany would build a real air force. Then he would be able to put his glider training to good use. He would be several steps ahead of other young men who would be signing up for pilots' training.

He resented the lack of flying opportunities, and his resentment of the anti-air-force clause in the Versailles treaty extended to other aspects of that treaty (which he really didn't understand) and to the politicians who had agreed to sign it. He listened to leaders of his Youth Group, who seemed to have simple solutions to Germany's problems. In a well-run country, his mother would not have to work, he was told. She would be at home taking care of him, being a *mother*, which is what a good German woman was supposed to do. What's more, the paper for which she was working was an unpatriotic rag, which supported all the evil men who had lost the war for Germany. It was made clear to Joachim that his mother, unconsciously of course, was working for Germany's enemies. She should not be blamed for what she did, for she was being influenced by all the clever, treacherous liberals around her, and she, herself, was just not intelligent or perceptive enough to understand what was happening. Eventually, she would learn what Joachim already knew: that soon there would be a free, strong and aggressive Germany with its own army and air force, respected and feared in the world. Meanwhile, he could work hard to make this dream come true. One way he could help was to listen to her conversation carefully, to pick up clues from the stories she told about the newspaper and its editorial decisions that might be helpful to the movement.

Joachim tried to listen more carefully to her conversation. Actually, he seemed to pick up little except some office gossip. But his troop leaders paid attention to what he had to say and occasionally took notes on his reports.

He considered this a very minor part of his Youth Movement activities. The regular meetings gave him a feeling of belonging that he had not had before. He tried to quit school to become a regular party employee, but was encouraged to continue his education. He would need mathematics, geography and physics for his flying career, he was told. And besides, when Hitler came into power, it would be important to know which teachers were "reliable" and which were "unpatriotic." He should also report on the actions and words of his teachers. Did they praise the current German government? Did they seem to be interested in the Nazi movement? Did they show a special interest in boys who might seem to be intelligent, but who were also Jewish? Again, his reports usually contained very little. His teachers were probably as unpolitical as those in most other German schools. But whatever he said was listened to carefully, and the obvious interest he aroused in his leaders gave him a feeling of importance.

The night of the torch parade, celebrating Hitler's rise to power, was the highpoint of Joachim's life. He had never felt so happy and fulfilled.

Looking back on that night now, he is appalled at how little he really knew about the movement to which he had intended to devote his life. "We were told what we wanted to hear," he said. "We were assured that we were important. Nobody else told German adolescents that they were important . . . ever. Certainly our parents and teachers didn't. We were also assured that, once Hitler was in power, all the wrongs we saw about us would be fixed, and that we would be allowed to help create a marvelous new country. When I marched in that parade, I thought it was only the beginning. I had been privileged to be an important person in helping to create the Thousand Year Reich, the great new Germany that Hitler would bring forth out of the chaos and trouble around us. I didn't know how he would do this. Nobody had ever spelled out any kind of program for us. We were just told to have faith. I had faith, and I had never been so exhilarated in my whole life."

FREEDOM DISAPPEARS SLOWLY

"It is of paramount interest to the state and the nation to prevent these people (i.e., the average German) from falling into the hands of bad, ignorant, or even vicious educators. The state, therefore has the duty of watching over their education and preventing any mischief. It must exercise strict control over the press; for its influence on these people is by far the strongest and most penetrating, since it is applied not once in a while, but over and over again. In the uniformity and constant repetition of its instruction lies its tremendous power. If anywhere, therefore, it is here that the state must not forget that all means must serve an end; it must not be confused by the drivel about the so-called 'freedom of the press' and let itself be taken into neglecting its duty and denying the nation the food which it needs and is good for it: with ruthless determination it must make sure of this instrument of popular education and place it in the service of the state and nation."

"If we do not lift the youth out of the morass of their present-day environment, they will drown in it. Anyone who refuses to see these things supports them, and thereby makes himself an accomplice in the slow prostitution of our future, which, whether we like it or not, lies in the coming generation. The cleansing of our culture must be extended to all fields.

Theater, art, literature, cinema, press, posters and window displays must be cleansed of all manifestations of our rotting world and placed in the service of moral, political and cultural ideas . . ."

—*Adolf Hitler in* MEIN KAMPF

"The media are the last institution in America which claims what is tantamount to the Divine Right of Kings. They have attacked and vilified virtually every other institution in society, demanding ever more public regulation while piously insisting that they should be free.

"Yet it is becoming increasingly apparent to many thoughtful citizens that this cannot go on. What is being perceived is that no government, whatever its ideological coloration, can hope to govern in an orderly and responsible manner when it is ceaselessly subjected to demagogic attacks against which there is no recourse . . .

"What destroys liberty, gentlemen of the press, is license, and I greatly fear that if you manage to encompass the destruction of Mr. Nixon you will find you have encompassed your own . . . and the verdict of the nation will be that you richly deserved it."

—*From a letter published in an American newspaper in 1974.*

Did our lives change suddenly the day in January 1933 that Hitler became the chancellor of Germany? If the answer to that question had been a simple "yes," the history of the world would probably have been quite different. Democracy in Germany (as in many other countries) did not vanish from one day to the next; it evaporated at first slowly and then at an increasingly faster pace.

"What happened was like a cancer," a German newspaper editor said. "The onset of the Nazi era was painless for most of us. Since there were so few symptoms that our freedoms were being eroded, only those who were immediately affected by seemingly arbitrary orders noticed what was happening. I noticed, because the newspaper on which my father worked was closed two days after Hitler came to power. A group of Brownshirts simply walked in and smashed the presses. My father could not get another job as a journalist, and went to work for a linotype company."

At first newspapers closed, magazines ceased publication, cabarets were padlocked because of so-called "spontaneous demonstrations of outraged citizens against un-German ideas and sentiments."

A little later all means of mass communication (the word "media" had not been invented in 1933, and there still is no exact German translation for it) were simply controlled by orders of the state. A newspaper was denied publication rights. The manuscript of a book was confiscated. A play that had been announced was just never performed. Certain commentators were no longer heard on the radio.

While all of this was happening, the constitution under which we all lived was never officially changed. That constitution, like its American counterpart, promised freedom of thought, religion, and of the press, and guaranteed German citizens certain rights, such as no arbitrary arrests, no unreasonable searches and seizures, free assembly and free association. Not only did Hitler not repeal the constitution of the Weimar Republic, he quoted it constantly. He used it to justify decrees that ran counter to both the spirit and the letter of basic German law. When he was accused of violating the constitution (while such accusations were still possible) he simply maintained that he understood the constitution better than the accuser, and he could always find a few lawyers who agreed with him.

There was indeed a provision in the German constitution that permitted the suspension of certain freedoms under emergency conditions (a fatal flaw, as many historians later noted).

It was this provision that Hitler persuaded the senile President Paul von Hindenburg to sign as a temporary measure. Hitler's reason for urging the suspension of liberties was the Reichstag (the German parliament building) fire. It went up in flames in February of 1933, just after Hitler became chancellor, and according to Hitler and his followers, the blaze had been caused by arson. Of course, the arsonists were left-wingers, he told Hindenburg, and Germany was in imminent danger of being taken over by the Communists. Many suspected that the fire had been set by the Nazis themselves as a perfect excuse to allow Hitler to rule under martial law. While the constitution was never repealed, neither was that so-called temporary emergency order, and it formed the basis for the flood of Hitler decrees, most of which were clearly unconstitutional.

"The first time the police broke down the door to our home at three in the morning, my father actually asked the men what right they had to come into our house without a court order," one German businessman whose father had been a labor leader said. "The police officers just laughed. 'Let's say our reason is that you're under suspicion,' one of them said. 'The next time we *won't* even have to suspect you . . . we just may not like you very much.'"

A physician's son told of his father's files being rifled by secret police in broad daylight, in the presence of his father, a nurse and a whole waiting room full of patients. "The only way we can find out whether Herr X's grandfather was Jewish is by looking at your records," they told the astonished doctor. "The Jews are a threat to our national security, and X is a teacher in a public school." Of course, the physician did not keep files on the religion of his patients' ancestors, but that did not keep the police from carting away X's file, plus several others. The physician complained and was informed that "national security matters" took precedence over his patients' personal privacy.

All of us who went to school began to notice that the contents of the books we read were changing. Of course, certain authors were banned entirely. In my own school we were asked to tape together two pages of our German literature anthology. They contained poems by one of Germany's outstanding nineteenth-century writers, Heinrich Heine, a Jew. The teacher came around and checked carefully to make sure we had taped the pages securely enough so we couldn't open them again. We received a new history book (there was too much "unGerman" material in our old one to make the taping process practical). Some teachers lost their jobs. If a student asked questions about the dismissal of a popular teacher, it was made clear that such an "unreasonable" attitude might affect the kind of recommendation the student would get to a university or for a job.

Looking back on the first months of the Hitler era, I feel it did not seem as if much that was happening affected our lives. When all humor disappeared from our favorite radio programs (that happened quickly—the Nazis realized very soon that laughter can be a potent weapon against dictatorship), we just listened to the radio less and played more records. If there were few good plays at the theater, we simply switched to motion pictures, preferably American ones. German movies at that time, like German theater, were almost invariably dull. They dealt with heroic youths who saved the town from the local Communist boss, usually sometime around 1929. Or they were biographies of newly discovered heroes, such as Frederick the Great (before they changed our history books he hadn't seemed all that great—rather a tyrannical, weak man, given to making damaging alliances and invading neighboring countries). On the other hand, American movies dealt with such fascinating subjects as Indians and settlers, gangsters and cops, or the beautiful young actress who rose to instant stardom in the Ziegfeld follies. We did not know that foreign motion pictures with any kind of social or political content were banned in Germany.

Some of our parents complained about the lack of real news in the press. But the scores of the local soccer team were still reported regularly, and certainly the headlines most of us scanned seemed more reassuring than they had formerly. There were fewer street fights, for instance, although few of us realized that what formerly was called "breaking and entering" or just plain "juvenile delinquency" was now often referred to as "a spontaneous demonstration of patriotic German youths." At any rate, we *saw* fewer fights. The "spontaneous demonstrations" during which liberal journalists, former labor leaders, cabaret artists and others were beaten up tended to occur at night, in dark alleys.

Perhaps many of us really noted for the first time on the evening of May 10, 1933 the hatred the Nazi bore against those who disagreed with them. On that night in Berlin, one of those "spontaneous demonstrations" broke out among university students. They started a torchlight parade (flaming torches by courtesy of the government were distributed) and marched to the university's front court. There a huge pile of books had been gathered, and the students threw their torches on it to set it on fire. More and more books from the university and other Berlin libraries were tossed into the flames. Dr. Joseph Goebbels (Hitler's Minister of Propaganda) just happened to be on the spot to give his blessing. "The soul of the German people can again express itself. Those flames not only illuminate the final end of an old era; they light up a new!" he cried.

Of course, other students and many librarians in other towns took the hint. The first book burning had been a headline event with not one editorial voice raised in protest. Subsequent conflagrations were mentioned on the back pages of newspapers and toward the end of radio newscasts.

A man who is now a professor of literature at a German university and who was a high school student at that time told of participating in the original book-burning ceremonies. "That was the biggest bonfire I had ever seen in our neighborhood . . . so, of course, I went," he said. "I hadn't heard of most of the writers whose books went up in flames. I knew who

Thomas Mann was, of course, but his long, complicated novels didn't interest me very much, although I couldn't quite understand why they seemed to upset Dr. Goebbels as much as they did. Of the foreign writers whose books were burned, I had read only some of Jack London's novels, and again, I couldn't understand why his stories of life in the arctic were 'un-German.' " Among the Americans who had their works added to the funeral pyre were Helen Keller (no one to this day understands why that happened, except as one student put it, "her name sounded Jewish") and Margaret Sanger (Hitler was known to disapprove of all forms of birth control).

Of course, the burning was only a symbolic gesture. All the books of which copies had been burned were subsequently banned from stores and libraries. Before the torchlight parade someone had put together a very careful list. It still seems strange to many of us who lived through the German book burnings that so many people become enraged when a book is *burned*, but not when it is *banned*. For instance, when, in 1974, a North Dakota school board banned Kurt Vonnegut's *Slaughterhouse Five* from the school library, the fact was not even reported in the American press until a school janitor, who simply did not know what to do with all those unwanted books, threw them into the school furnace. It was at that point that the story made national news.

At any rate, as books disappeared from schools, libraries, and the bookshelves in the homes of good Nazis, people simply read less. Reading wasn't one of the activities that was especially encouraged for young people anyhow. Active sports were.

Nazi ideas, and Hitler's personal preferences, were soon apparent in other fields besides literature. Hitler considered himself an artist and an art critic. He insisted on photographic realism . . . and imposed his tastes on the German art world. A special museum, *Das Haus der Deutschen Kunst* (The House of German Art), opened in Munich to show the work of approved German painters and sculptors. It abounded in paintings of brown-shirted Hitler Youths gazing raptly at the sky or at a German flag, sturdy German peasants digging the soil, and idealized German mothers with at least eight children, all blond and blue-eyed. Apparently the museum bored most German art lovers (non-art lovers don't go to museums much in any case). It was always empty.

On the other hand, Dr. Goebbels, in order to show the Germans the kind of artistic horrors from which they were being saved, opened another art show almost across the street from *Das Haus der Deutschen Kunst*. The "Exhibition of Forbidden Art," which showed the work of some of the world's greatest contemporary painters and sculptors, taken from German museums and galleries, was an instantaneous success. The lines around the exhibit were even longer than around the motion picture theaters that showed American films. The contrast in attendance between the two art exhibits so annoyed Dr. Goebbels that he had the "Forbidden" art show closed, and ordered the paintings and drawings sold. Many of them were snapped up by lucky foreign collectors who paid a few hundred marks for a Picasso or a Paul Klee that would be worth over $100,000 twenty years later. Germans, of course, would not have dared to buy any of those paintings, even those Germans who loved and appreciated the artists. By that time, one did not want to get one's name on an official record as wishing to own a painting of which Hitler disapproved.

As books disappeared from bookstores, magazine publishing houses were closed, newspapers censored and political humor banned from radio and the cabaret, a few Germans became increasingly unhappy. But these were the same people who had always objected to censorship, and who could contemptuously be dismissed by the government as "dissatisfied intellectuals" or "pacifist troublemakers" or "bourgeois liberals." Most Germans accepted the official explanation that books had to be censored and "cleansed of pornography" to uplift the morals of German youth, that newspapers had to be stopped from printing "slanderous untruths about their government" or "items that put the leadership of Germany in a bad light," that theater and radio were supposed to be "educational tools" and that making light of serious matter or being critical of government policy was somehow unpatriotic.

There were those who had always regarded the press with suspicion, especially the part of the press that was critical of the status quo. These people were delighted that "such trash" was no longer published. Only a minority of Germans had read the books and magazines that were banned in any case. Looking back, it seems that most of us heard fewer complaints about the banning of books, theater, art, films and censorship of the press than we heard about the fact that butter was being replaced on grocery shelves with a particularly bad-tasting form of margarine. Interestingly enough, the margarine soon disappeared and butter returned. One wonders what would have happened if instead of complaining about the taste of the margarine, more adults had started to complain seriously about the Nazis' taste in the arts and about the censorship that was stifling all freedom of expression.

When *people* started to disappear, many more Germans became suspicious and unhappy. At first, the disappearances were quite official. For instance, when the chief editorial writer for a newspaper in my mother's hometown of Essen was sent to jail for "false and malicious attacks on the government and party" even a few of those who approved of official censorship of news shook their heads. "I can understand confiscating the paper if it isn't printing the truth, but just because a reporter got a story wrong, is that a reason for sending him to jail?" was the kind of remark one heard about the incident. Few people seemed to feel that the story might actually have been *correct.*

There were a number of such arrests, with jail sentences becoming longer and longer. (The editorial writer on the Essen paper had received only a two-month term.) Eventually, of course, such public criticism would lead not to the city's main prison for a month or so, but to a concentration camp and even to summary execution. It might still have been possible to organize an effective protest the first time an editor was jailed, if enough Germans had been interested. It became impossible as Hitler and his secret police took increasing control over all aspects of German life. Any attempt at organization would have been stopped before it started.

In 1934 people started to disappear with no official explanation being given. Their friends and relatives would search for them, would try to find out from the police or local party headquarters what had happened, and would usually be given vague answers such as: "Mr. X has been arrested for his own protection. No, we don't know when he'll be allowed to come back." The people who disappeared were usually journalists, former government officials, leaders of the old opposition parties and others who might be expected to lead a protest against the increasingly repressive measures of the government.

The Nazi party was exceedingly efficient at rooting out potential opposition before it happened, and eliminating prospective organizers of protests. The bravest were frequently those who were arrested first, to make sure that those with less courage and determination would heed the warning signals and remain quiet.

The Nazis did not have the kind of sophisticated recording and bugging equipment that is available today. They tended to use human, rather than electronic, spies to watch potential troublemakers. Everyone suspected that he or she was being spied on, sometimes officially, by the so-called party block wardens, sometimes unofficially, by employers, employees, and occasionally even close friends and relatives. By 1936 almost everyone I knew was careful about what he or she said. I was warned by my parents, for instance, not to tell my closest friend that we were planning to leave Germany. It was difficult to convince myself that she would report any conversation with me to a party warden, and even more difficult to meet her for the last time without letting her know that I might never see her again, but I did as I was told. When, more than two decades later, I tried to find that friend, one of the reasons for my search was that I felt I owed her an apology. Of course, she would not have told! As it turned out, she probably would have. By the time we left, she was already deeply involved in the Nazi Youth Movement, a former teacher told me. She eventually rose to a top position in the National Socialist Women's Movement, was tried before a denazification court, and was sentenced to five years in prison. There is no way of knowing for sure if she would have betrayed us—but then there never was, with anyone. The unofficial, but well organized, spy system was cleverly used to undermine trust in one's fellow citizens. When trust in one's neighbors is gone, the totalitarian state has almost accomplished the ultimate control of everyone's life, because speaking out to anyone, anywhere, could be dangerous.

There are reasons why so many Germans accepted this control. It was the price they paid for more order, less unemployment, more opportunities for fun and recreation for those who toed the line.

There were those who had always believed that freedom leads to license, that patriotism means an uncritical attitude toward the state, and finally, that the leadership of that state should not be subjected to public scrutiny. "They know something that we don't. After all they are running the government," was a reason that was frequently given when disturbing news of new arrests, or the closing of newspapers and theaters was reported. "We might not think that Herr X is a danger to the state . . . he looks harmless enough to us . . . but Hitler must know, or he would not have had him arrested."

In the first years of the Nazi era, life was easier and more pleasant for many Germans, and they considered the sacrifice of civil liberties a small one when it meant a secure job and enough food on the table. Those who reported their neighbors for "antisocial" acts often did so out of a firm conviction that they were doing their duty as good citizens.

By the time many Germans (perhaps most of them) began to realize that they were prisoners of their government, that the officials, whose salaries were paid by the citizens' taxes, had arbitrary powers that ranged from control of food and employment to control of life and death, it was too late. When protest can mean death, who has the courage to lift his or her voice? A few did and paid with their lives. Most remained silent. Democracy had slipped away—apparently beyond recall.

But then, democracy in Germany had always been a rather shaky proposition—or so a great many people said later on.

"TOMORROW BELONGS TO ME"

The sun in the meadow is summery warm,
The stag in the forest runs free—
The heart as a shelter defies the storm
Tomorrow belongs to me.

The branch in the linden is leafy and green
The rage has deserted the sea;
The world holds a promise that shines unseen
Tomorrow belongs to me.

> —Lyrics for the song
> "TOMORROW BELONGS TO ME"
> by Fred Ebb from the musical CABARET.

Now is the time
The hour calls to action
To cut down evil
To bring about a new world

Where every man on earth will have a good life and home.

On the horizon we see a bright light.
The earth is turning to a new and better future.

As false gods fall
All men will be free . . .

Lyrics from JEZT IST DIE ZEIT *as reproduced*
in the Hitler Youth Song Book
lyrics by Christian Lahusen, 1931.

"It all sounded not only harmless but beautiful. Youth leading the way to a better world for all mankind. That's what we were told we could do. We were the important ones. We had not been corrupted by the old values. We could understand." That's how one sad, gray German postal clerk recalled his early membership in the Hitler Youth.

In the motion picture *Cabaret* (which uses the location and the performers in a shoddy Berlin nightclub to symbolize the decline and fall of the German Republic) a young, proud and beautiful boy stands in the garden of a Bavarian country inn singing, "Tomorrow Belongs to Me." There is no hate, not even grim determination on his face; only joy and dedication to the new and better world he is describing. One by one the other guests at the inn join his song: mothers and fathers lifting their children to their shoulders, workers putting their tool kits under the table, women pushing aside their coffee cups or beer steins as they rise to their feet. Only a very few elderly people remain silent. Most of these look indifferent and some skeptical. One man bangs his beer stein on the table and moves his chair, obviously disgusted by the scene. As the camera moves away from the garden and the inn, one of the film's principal characters, a young British university instructor, asks another character, a German aristocrat, "Are you really sure you can control these people?" The aristocrat had assured the instructor earlier as they watched the aftermath of a bloody battle between a group of Nazi storm troopers and a Communist youth organization, that he, personally, welcomed civic disorder. His point was that the Communists and the Nazis would wipe each other out, and then he and people like him (responsible conservative Germans) would, of course, take over the power to which they had always been entitled.

The scene in the beer garden, superficially beautiful and peaceful, made many of us who grew up in Germany in the 1930s shudder as we watched the film. In many ways it was much more frightening than some of the violence in *Cabaret* (the stomping to death of the cabaret owner who refused to allow members of the Nazi party to enter his establishment to solicit funds, or the bloody body of a puppy with its throat cut deposited on the front doorstep of the dog's owner, a Jewish girl). Almost everyone who lived in Germany during the last years of the Weimar Republic and the early years of the Nazi era, knew many young, proud, idealistic, convinced Hitler followers. If you were young, often the most popular, friendliest, most helpful of your classmates wore the red flag with the white center and the black swastika, either as a lapel pin or as an armband. Because these boys and girls were so convinced themselves, they could be very persuasive. Because they were so thoroughly idealistic, and frequently such good friends, they actually persuaded a number of their classmates and, occasionally, even a teacher to join them.

Looking back at my own junior-high-school class, I remember one girl, Ruth, who was always chosen for every elective office. Of course, we had no student government; the whole concept of students running their own affairs was entirely foreign to the German educational system in those days. But Ruth felt that we *should* have a large voice in the kind of courses we had to take, our athletic progam, after-school activities, and a way to present our grievances against some of the teachers. So, she was elected to head every club, every team, every committee. Her most appealing qualities were her total sincerity and her willingness to share whatever she had with a classmate in need. If the school was cold because of a temporary coal shortage (they occurred often in those days, when miners went on strike), Ruth would always lend you her sweater; she insisted that the cold air made her feel more alive. If you forgot your lunch, Ruth shared hers; she was not very hungry that day. Out of the same generosity that promoted her to share her clothing and her food, she also shared her ideas. Ruth was a totally dedicated Nazi.

She always had a large number of pamphlets, booklets, newsletters and other materials in her book bag, along with her school supplies. She never seemed to force the conversation toward politics. If one wanted to discuss clothes or one's problem with a teacher or a parent with Ruth, she was always willing to do so. But somehow, the discussion tended to turn political. Clothes really shouldn't matter so much. In the new and better Germany everyone would have a sufficient wardrobe, but clothes would no longer be a status symbol, she would say. Unfair teachers were another symbol of German decadence, she maintained. Teachers had been directed to prefer some students to others. Many were more interested in advancing their careers than in preparing young Germans for the future that lay ahead. And parents, of course, were old-fashioned, with outdated values and ideas. This was not their fault. They, too, had been exposed to all the nonsense the government had drummed into their heads through the educational system, the press, and their own misguided parents. Eventually these problems would all be solved through a new and radical system. "Here, take this booklet, it will explain what I'm talking about," she would often say, pressing into our hands yet another piece of literature, which often seemed surprisingly relevant to the problem we had been discussing. Because Ruth rarely argued, almost never lost her temper, always listened and was often ready to supply practical help as well as pamphlets, many of us read the Nazi propaganda with a lot more concentration than we might have, had Ruth been less attractive than she was.

Some of us, especially those of us who were called "non-Aryan" (and therefore, thoroughly evil) in Ruth's booklets, often asked her how she could possibly have friends who were Jews or who had a Jewish background, when everything she read and distributed seemed to breathe hate against us and our ancestors. "Of course, they don't mean *you*," she would explain earnestly. "You are a good German. It's those other Jews, pacificists, socialists and liberals who betrayed Germany, that Hitler wants to remove from influence. You, like me, will be part of the better life, when the school won't be cold anymore because the miners will get enough money so they won't have to strike."

When Hitler actually came to power and the word went out that students of Jewish background were to be isolated, that "Aryan" Germans were no longer to associate with "non-Aryan" (i.e., those who were either Jewish or who had one Jewish ancestor, even though they themselves were Christians), Ruth actually came around and apologized to those of us to whom she was no longer able to talk. "The whole thing may be a misunderstanding," she explained. "Maybe it will all be straightened out later. But meanwhile, Hitler must know what he is doing, and I'll follow orders." Not only did she no longer speak to the suddenly ostracized group of classmates, she carefully noted down anybody who did, and reported them. She was, of course, selected to be the leader of her Hitler Youth Girls Troop, just as she had always been elected to head any group to which she belonged. Most of us who had been so fond of her in the days when she explained that we were *good Germans*, were more puzzled than angry. She didn't seem to have changed at all, only the circumstances under which she operated had changed.

Years later, after the war, some of us who had left Germany before being a non-Aryan became a danger to one's life checked on what had become of Ruth in the intervening decades. Miraculously, our school had not been hit by a bomb, and records were still intact.

Ruth had graduated from high school, joined the Nazi Women's organization after she outgrew the Girls Troop and had gone to nursing school. In a letter to our old headmistress she had written that "she had always loved people, and nursing seemed an especially valuable way to serve the new Germany." However, there were some other records available on her activities. She had eventually become a nurse in a concentration camp where so-called experiments were carried out on helpless inmates. Most of these inmates died after appalling suffering. The headmistress, who like most of us had liked and admired Ruth, shook her head when she told us that Ruth had eventually been brought before a denazification court and accused and convicted of crimes against humanity. "In some ways it's hard to believe that she could have done those terrible things," the headmistress said. "But thinking back, I see now that Ruth had very little imagination. She really cared more about her beliefs and ideas than she did about people. Did you know that she reported one of our teachers, one she admitted she liked a lot, for making a joke about Hitler? The teacher lost his job here and could never find another one. I discussed this man's fate with her, and she said that she was deeply sorry for him and his family . . . but traitors just had to be eliminated from the educational system. She must have become convinced that the 'experiments' were more important to the new Germany than the suffering of the people who endured them. She really wasn't a sadist, she was not really a bad person, she was what I call an ideologue. Once she had come to believe in an idea—no matter how perverted, illogical and evil—she couldn't let go. She's now in prison and she's probably still sure that what she believed was right . . . something just went wrong along the way with the manner in which her ideas were carried out."

Those of us who have met and seen such ideologues now recognize them. The beautiful, proud, dedicated young boy who sang "Tomorrow Belongs to Me" presented the perfect picture of an ideologue (he was a great actor). That's why he made so many of us shudder with fear.

WHAT OTHERS REMEMBER: VOICES FROM MUNICH AND BERLIN 1930-1936

"A wolf has been born, destined to hurl itself on the herds of seducers and deceivers of the people."

> —Adolf Hitler, *writing in the* VOELKISCHER BEOBACHTER, *the official newspaper of the Nazi party.*

The thread that runs through almost all the interviews with Germans who are now middle-aged, but who were in their teens during the time when Hitler rose to power, is distrust. Most, of course, reported how their parents felt about events in Germany during the crucial years between 1930 and 1936. However, frequently their own feelings only echoed those of their families.

Usually, the distrust produced indifference. Most Germans simply didn't want to become involved. They considered all politicians as corrupt or corruptible, newspapers as biased, political speeches as empty promises, and the ever-present street fights in the major cities as the battles of rowdies and hoodlums.

"I heard on the radio almost every day that Nazis and Communists were waging bloody battles in Berlin," said one woman, whom we shall call Hilda, who was a teenager during the last years of the Weimar Republic. "The father of a friend was a policeman. He said he would just stand by and let those hoods kill each other off—the fewer of them there were around, the less trouble there would be next year. Most of us agreed with that statement. Certainly my parents did. They saw very little difference between the warring factions. We just assumed that everyone who had fights with the Nazis were Communists. Of course, as it turned out, that wasn't true. The Nazis would break up or try to break up any meeting of any group that disagreed with them."

Hilda, of course, didn't understand that Hitler, himself, was well aware of the drama that the fights created, and that they got for him much needed free space in the press. Hitler was also aware of the distrust of politics and government by most Germans, like Hilda's parents and the policemen.

"The party was in its infancy. It had not yet been tested, and Hitler was anxious that it should receive a baptism of fire. He wanted a large hall and a large audience, preferably including a fair proportion of Communists, and above all, he wanted drama and excitement. He had come to the simple conclusion that a speech would be remembered more vividly if accompanied by violence. He therefore welcomed violent interruptions, because they gave his bodyguards an excuse to wade through the crowd and engage in savage fighting," reported Robert Payne, in his book, *The Life and Death of Adolf Hitler.*

Of course, political leaders, before and since the Hitler years, have used similar techniques to attract attention to otherwise not too memorable speeches. For instance, one presidential assistant at the time of the 1972 election in the United States commented in the margin of a Secret Service document that forewarned of disturbances at a Republican rally, "Good" and "Great." However, Hitler raised this particular attention-getting device to a fine art.

If the average German was disgusted with the fighting and chaos, Hitler was getting his name in the papers, and his followers were proud of him.

He had another trick that he used frequently to call attention to himself. A Berlin banker who went to his first party meeting at the age of seventeen (and who insists that he never went to another one voluntarily) remembers that there was a series of spectacularly boring speakers preceding Hitler. "Everybody spoke in mild and general terms, attacked nobody, and one even thanked the Communists in the audience for listening so politely. Then Hitler came striding into the hall (he made it a point to be late) and gave one of his thundering orations. He spoke of the degradation, disunity, crime and violence that, he insisted, the democratic government was encouraging, either deliberately or through its permissiveness. Then he launched into a shining vision of a new Germany, free of traitors, weaklings, pacifists, Communists, pornographers, decadent intellectuals and Jews. Of course, he was heckled, and his followers waded into the crowd to silence the hecklers. After Hitler left, a real brawl broke out, with police dragging both attackers and attacked off to jail. I got out quietly by the back door. Getting arrested in that kind of fight seemed like a very bad idea. For one thing, my parents would have been appalled. For another, the whole meeting seemed so pointless."

Of course, that meeting and hundreds of others like it, called by Hitler or one of his principal assistants, were not pointless at all. Those who listened to Hitler's speeches fairly regularly (because they believed in him, or because they were just interested) remark now that he always seemed to be saying the same things, reciting the same facts, making the same accusations, even using the same tone of voice: starting calmly and quietly, and then rising to almost hysterical violence. Newspapers began to report simply that Hitler had made "his speech," assuming that their readers probably knew the content. However, even this was calculated. Early in his career, Hitler had learned that his audiences were not interested in closely reasoned ideas. What they liked was pounding repetition: the same attacks against the liberals, the Jews, the press and the pacifists, using the same frightening and passionate phrases, with the same promises of a great and bright future.

If he spoke in Bavaria, where he had a strong following, he would pour special scorn on the government in Berlin, using the prejudices of the Bavarians against the Prussians, usually with very good effect. Then, when he spoke in Berlin, he concentrated on the power of the big landowners, the department store managers who kept prices up and who, according to him, spouted liberal ideas to fool the people, the international bankers and the Communists (who, according to him, were mostly Jewish), who were trying to take over Germany and destroy the fine, hardworking, upstanding citizen with their schemes and plots.

"One man, who looked like a student, asked at the meeting I attended why the Communists and the international bankers were working together," a man who is now a banker reported. "That seemed like a fairly intelligent question to me, but one of Hitler's guards just walked up to him and hit him in the mouth. The police stood by doing nothing."

People who lived in Munich during these years remember that very frequently the police would watch a bloody battle from the sidelines. They probably agreed with Hilda's policeman father that both parties to the violence were scum, who might as well finish each other off. But the Nazis were often better armed and better prepared than the people they attacked. The bloody heads often belonged to newspaper reporters, university students or others who generally had not sought the fight. "We sometimes got the impression that the police were neutral on the side of the Nazis," one Bavarian who got caught in the middle of such a fight in 1932 said. "I certainly had no intention of attacking those brown-shirted giants. I was rather small and slight, wore glasses and was carrying my books home in a satchel from high school. They jumped me. The police didn't stop them until they had broken my glasses, given me a bloody nose and had me down on the ground, kicking my ribs. I thought they would kill me. Then one of the

police officers said: 'Oh, let the guy alone . . . he's had enough.
He won't get into trouble again.' Everybody laughed, and the
Nazis took off. I went to a doctor's office and had my ribs taped
up."
   The same man admits that six months later, he, too, joined
the party. He also says that he doesn't remember now why he
did it.
   There is a woman in a small town near Bonn. Most of her
friends belonged to the local Hitler Youth Group by 1932.
She tried to join, "much as you'd want to join any group,"
she says. She attended several meetings and had a glorious time
going on hikes, singing patriotic songs, sitting around campfires at night. One afternoon her leader told her, rather apolo-
getically, that she was no longer welcome. Someone (she never
learned who) had reported that one of her great-grandparents
had been a converted Jew. "We'll have to consider you politi-
cally unreliable," the leader explained. The rejected girl spent
months going through family Bibles and other records trying
to prove that the accusation was not true and that she was as
qualified to be a good Nazi as any other girl in the neighborhood. "When we moved to Munich, I tried to join up again.
But my records had managed to follow me," she said. Although she now seems to understand something about the
true nature of the organization she so desperately wanted to
join then, she still speaks with some bitterness about the
"enemy" in her hometown who reported her "racial undesira-
bility" to her troop leader. Incidentally, her great-grandmother's Jewish background was apparently never entirely
proved, because it caused her no further trouble. She was able
to attend a university and to become a teacher. And to this
day, the thought that her great-grandmother might indeed
have been Jewish brings forth a stream of indignant denials.
"Obviously nobody ever could prove it," she says with a certain
amount of pride.
   One of the best records of that time appears in a German
book long out of print, written after World War II by Melita

Maschmann. The book is called *Fazit*, a legal term, meaning something like "brief" or "answer to an indictment." Miss Maschman wrote her book as an explanation to a Jewish classmate. She discussed why she had become involved in the Hitler Youth early in its formation, had risen to power first in the Youth Movement and then in the Women's Movement, and had refused, even at the end of the war, to believe the horrible t th about the destruction of 6 million innocent Jewish men, women and children.

She wrote of her youthful indignation at the "unfairness" of life in Germany. Her parents apparently belonged to the upper middle class. They had servants. She felt that one person should not be compelled to wait on another. The parents were materialistic. She felt that one should devote one's life to goals higher than making money or getting into the right schools and universities. Her father cared very much for his reputation. She felt that this frequently led to hypocrisy, that honesty and self-sacrifice should be the leading themes in her life. She says in her book that she truly loved Germany, not as an abstraction, but as a concrete reality: she loved the pine woods, the lakes, the sandy, infertile soil of the area where she lived, the mountains, valleys and streams of the town they visited on their vacations. Germany to her was not a country in the national sense of the word, but a series of landscapes filled with sights, sounds and smells that meant home to her. She became convinced that this home was threatened, and that the way to fight that threat was to join with other dedicated young people, a movement dedicated to the preservation of all she felt to be vitally important.

She points out that she was so unaware of what the Hitler Movement was really about that she urged her Jewish friend (to whom the book is dedicated) to join the Youth Group with her, and was hurt that the other girl turned her down.

But with great honesty, she admits that as she rose to power in the Women's Movement, she began to understand how much evil was mixed with all that idealism. She says that she often told herself that the end (a free, just and strong Germany) justified the means. Eventually, she had to admit to herself that her actions no longer even had very much connection with her ideals. But she had gained so much power and recognition that she could not give up the position she had achieved. She was as concerned with her reputation as her father had been, and her status had been achieved by means considerably more dishonest and immoral than anything her family had ever done.

It would have been interesting to talk to Miss Maschmann. However, by 1972 her book was available only in one library in Munich. Her publisher did not even have a copy. Nor could he tell me where she could be found. He was able to produce the address of her brother, and the brother insisted that the last he had heard of his sister, she had gone to India and was working in an orphanage. She had given up writing, was out of contact with her family, and her family was out of contact with her. Others in the town in which she had spent her childhood, and who were probably among her comrades in that Youth Group about which she wrote so enthusiastically, refused to discuss her or their own experiences. As far as everyone who knew her was concerned, Melita Maschmann, who wrote an honest, convincing book about the motives of a youngster who joined the Nazi party as a gesture of idealism and remained in it because of a drive for raw power, might have disappeared from the face of the earth.

Germans loved to see their very unromantic looking Führer in romantic poses. Pictures like this could be seen on the walls of many German homes.

Hitler's love of little children and animals was one of the qualities the German Propaganda Ministry emphasized at every opportunity. It was hard to find a newspaper in Germany in 1933 that didn't feature at least one picture of Hitler with a child or a dog . . . or both. Over 2 million children died in his concentration camps before the end of World War II.   COURTESY NATIONAL ARCHIVES

Little Helga Goebbels, the daughter of Hitler's Propaganda Minister, was also often photographed with Der Führer. A few years later she was poisoned, at Hitler's and her parents' orders, in the bunker under Berlin, as Russian troops closed in on the city. So were her five brothers and sisters. Her parents committed suicide a few hours later.

Das Haus Der Deutschen Kunst was one of the buildings Hitler helped to design personally. It contained the kind of superpatriotic bad art he loved. He had wanted to become an architect and had been denied admission to the university architecture school because he could not meet admissions standards. He blamed the "Jewish academic establishment" for his frustrated ambitions.

Superhighways (Autobahnen) and aqueducts were among Hitler's proudest early accomplishments. They relieved unemployment immediately and later served to transport war material, as Germany invaded neighboring countries. Still, today, some German will say: "Yes, Hitler did a lot of terrible things . . . but don't forget, he built the Autobahn."

Perhaps one of the most important sources of enthusiastic support for Hitler among many Germans was the creation of the new, modern German air force, also in clear violation of the Versailles treaty. Bombs from these planes were to destroy most major European cities less than a decade later. In a time when it was still possible to stop Germany from building them, world leaders did nothing.

Another source of pride to many Germans was that Hitler, contrary to the provisions of the Versailles treaty, built a great, new navy. The world leaders knew that the treaty provisions were being broken . . . but no one did anything about the breach, except to write an occasional feeble protest.

Political training began at a young age. These children have joined their first organized Hitler Youth program. They are six years old.

Military training started early in Hitler's Germany. It was part of the many "games" played by Hitler Youth troops on their camping trips and marches.

Men were stacked, like pieces of firewood, in Germany's many concentration camps. These were lucky ... they survived to be liberated by American soldiers at the end of the war. More than 6 million other men, women and children died. COURTESY NATIONAL ARCHIVES

In 1933, the signs read: GERMANS! DEFEND YOURSELVES! DON'T BUY FROM JEWS! *Nobody explained why anyone needed a defense against a Jewish-owned hardware store, but the grim looking storm troopers at the store's door were usually enough to make the potential customer walk around the block to find an "Aryan" dealer.*

COURTESY NATIONAL ARCHIVES

A Berlin landmark, the Kaiser Wilhelm Gedächtniskirche, a Protestant church, as photographed in 1930.

The same church, as photographed in 1946. It has been left standing in its present condition to remind Germans of the ruin the Hitler years created, in their own country and in the countries his armies invaded and destroyed. COURTESY GERMAN INFORMATION CENTER

One of the central squares in Berlin in 1930, the Pottsdammer Platz, a commercial center. Most of the buildings in the picture were destroyed by bombs. COURTESY GERMAN INFORMATION CENTER

Hitler, with two of the children of his Propaganda Minister, Joseph Goebbels. Goebbels and his wife Magda had six children. All died, poisoned by their parents, in a bunker under Berlin as the Russian armies closed in. The parents committed suicide, right after Hitler and the wife he had married a few hours earlier took their own lives.

COURTESY NATIONAL ARCHIVES

"WE CANNOT HELP OURSELVES ANYMORE"

"We cannot help ourselves or you anymore!
We cannot help ourselves or you anymore!"

—*The final lines in the opera* MAHAGONNY, *written by Bertold Brecht and Kurt Weill, two of Germany's outstanding artists, who left their country in 1933. The opera opened in September 1930, shortly after the election that gave Hitler 6.5 million votes.*

Mahagonny is an opera with a political message whose final implications few in the audience understood at the time it opened. Mahagonny is not a color, not a person, but a mythical city. It's a modern version of Sodom and Gomorrah, a place where everything is permitted to those who have money to pay for their sins, and a city in which God himself finally appears and tells everybody to "go to Hell," literally. One critic described it as a play that makes the point that men don't understand and probably, therefore, don't deserve freedom.

Among those who made the journey to Leipzig to see the opening performance of the opera, was a sixteen-year-old Berlin high-school student, Kurt, whose father was a stage designer and who, himself, wanted to become an actor. "My parents were very liberal," he said. "I was allowed to read and see anything they felt I could understand. That was considered very un-German by all our friends and neighbors. Certainly most of my teachers disapproved. They thought that my parents' permissiveness would turn me into an immoral, perverted adult."

Kurt remembers that his father, who had sometimes designed sets for Brecht, was very excited about the opera's opening. "In fact, he was so excited he hardly listened to the radio for election returns." When he found out the turn the vote had taken, however, he agreed to let his son miss school to attend the opera. "There may not be very many more plays like this in Germany," he said.

They traveled to Leipzig and attended a dress rehearsal. Outside the theater crowds of brown-shirted men carried placards protesting the opening. Kurt remembers asking one of the pickets if he knew what the opera was about, or if he had ever seen any of Brecht's or Weill's work. "Of course not!" the man answered indignantly. "I wouldn't consider going to see such dirt. It's pornography, that's what it is." Before Kurt could ask how the man knew this, since he clearly hadn't ever been near any of the work he condemned, Kurt's father grabbed him by the arm and took him into the theater. "It's not safe to argue with those people," he said. This was one of the minor surprises the visit held for Kurt. In his family, one argued about *everything*. Disagreements sharpened one's wits. One might yell at another, one might express one's opinions in very strong terms, but one didn't take that kind of argument personally. Kurt didn't realize how exceptional his family really was until much later.

The dress rehearsal was conducted in a threatening atmosphere, he reports. No one was entirely sure that the work would be allowed to open, as more and more uniformed men appeared around the theater. On opening night, the audience overflowed the auditorium. But it was obvious from the beginning that, although many had come to listen and to find out what the much-discussed opera was all about, others had come with the firm intention of disrupting the performance. "It was often impossible to hear what was said on the stage, with all the shouting, booing and whistling," Kurt said. "By the time the last act had started, fistfights had broken out in the audience. Before the play was finished, my father took me out of the theater." There was a riot in progress, and Kurt's father feared for their safety.

As it turned out, that was the last regular performance of the opera. The next one was given with the house lights on and corps of uniformed police lining the walls. Nor were there many more performances, either in Leipzig or anywhere else. It had become quite unsafe to perform an opera, a play, a film or, for that matter, to give an art show of which the Nazi party disapproved. Artists, performers and audiences could count on mobs of brown-shirted men with picket signs and/or clubs showing up at such events. All it took was a bad notice in one of the Nazi party papers. And in those days notices appeared before, not after, the opening. The picket to whom Kurt had spoken in Leipzig was certainly not alone in wishing to censor material he had never seen or heard.

When Kurt got back to school, he didn't tell anyone, not even his best friend, that he had gone to Leipzig with his father to see the controversial opera. He had already learned one lesson: in the time and place in which he lived, one did not admit to having controversial ideas or doing controversial things. For him, such an admission might end in a serious black mark on his school record, barring him from the university. So he just told everybody that he had been in bed with a bad cold. He didn't want to lie, but he had also learned that lies were sometimes necessary if one wished to stay out of serious trouble. As he grew older, Kurt found lying increasingly difficult. The basic openness and honesty of his childhood home got in the way of constant pretense. He spent three years in the concentration camp, Dachau, because of his final inability to stop disagreeing, to keep his opinions to himself, to nod, to smile and to greet his neighbors with a raised arm and a friendly "Heil Hitler," when required.

Those who like Kurt's parents were used to questioning feelings and events, asked themselves and others in those September days of 1930: "What has happened to us?" They didn't understand the large vote for a party that seemed to have its basis in hate and fear, and they didn't understand the sudden intolerance of some forms of literature, art and music; most of all they didn't understand why some of the brightest and best of the German intellectuals were beginning to talk of leaving the country.

More than forty years later historians are still asking: "What happened?" There are hundreds of answers to that question, and none really seems to satisfy even a majority of those who ask it. Some of those who were in their teens during the early 1930s provide only partial explanations.

"The reason why so many of my friends were not allowed to read certain books, see certain plays and movies or even ask questions about them at the dinner table, might give a clue to their parents' state of mind," Kurt said. "Those parents were frightened. They had certain values like thrift, hard work, and patriotism. These values were being questioned, it seemed to them, not only by the so-called intellectuals and the liberal press, but even by events. Inflation seemed to prove that thrift would not always assure security. Unemployment showed that hard work was not always rewarded. Germany had lost a world war and no matter how hard the people tried to convince themselves that the loss had been caused by cowards and traitors on the home front, they still had doubts. In a world where all foundations rock, people look for safe opinions, simple ideas, basic feelings. It's always safe to praise old virtues; nationalism and patriotism are very simple ideas; and hate always has been a basic feeling. Of course, so has love. But, somehow, when life gets tough, it's easier to hate than to love."

Most other reasons given by Germans who are adults today

and were teenagers when the surprising swing to Hitler took place, are similar to Kurt's.

"There were so many things going wrong in our country," says Hedwig, looking back. "My father could not find a job . . . that, of course, for us was more important than anything else. We couldn't blame my father . . . we knew, that although he was a very difficult man, who had had all kinds of problems getting along with employers and coworkers for years, he was really trying. So, when he told us that there was a conspiracy to keep him and other 'good Germans' like him down, and that the conspirators were the Jews, the liberal press, the Communists and their sympathizers, we believed him. Hitler would, somehow in some way, stop the influence that all those conspirators were having on our lives. So we supported Hitler."

Günter Grass, one of the world's outstanding novelists, was only three years old in 1930. He lived in Danzig. In his book *From the Diary of a Snail*, he tells about a parade he heard about later that passed "through the inner city in the morning and through the suburb of Langfuhr in the afternoon until, grown tired under placards and banners, the parade crowded into the Klein Hammerpark Garden restaurant. The concluding speech featured the motto: 'The Jews are our misfortune!' Some of the newspapers called it impressive."

Grass also describes how harmless and sunny the parade seemed to those who participated. "Nothing special: a parade for a purpose among other parades for other purposes. No dead or wounded, no property damage. Only increased beer consumption and merriment verging on the staggers. [What they sang then: 'Cornflowers blue . . .'] Lots of young people in their Sunday best, flowery summer dresses, a folk festival."

Grass then summarizes as only a superb writer can, the undercurrent of that meeting. "Since everyone knows fears, and wants to avoid misfortune, everyone was glad to hear misfortune called at last by its name, to know at last where the high prices, unemployment, housing shortage and private stomach ulcers came from. At the Klein Hammerpark, under the chestnut trees, it was easy to say all that out loud. There was [is] a Klein Hammerpark everywhere. Consequently, the meaning was not: the Danzig Jews are our misfortune. But the Jews in general, everywhere. Wherever a handy name was sought for misfortune, it was found: in Frankfurt, in Bielefeld, Leipzig, Karlsruhe, Danzig and Kleve . . ."

The name for misfortune was "Jews." At the end of World War II someone tried to take a census of the Jewish community in Danzig. Of the 10,448, there were less than 20 left. Some had emigrated to Palestine . . . fewer to America. The vast majority were dead. This was obviously not the way that those gay paraders had expected their folk festival to end.

In discussing the Günter Grass story with me, Kurt reminisced about another kind of parade he had seen only a year or so ago on a German television channel. On Wall Street, New York City, the United States of America, a group of construction workers with signs about TRAITORS, COWARDS, and LONG-HAIRED PEACENICKS had attacked a group of protesters (against the war in Vietnam) with chains, clubs and fists. Not only had they not been arrested, he pointed out, but "their leaders were invited to your White House." "Perhaps those men too felt that: 'We cannot help ourselves or you anymore,' " he said. "Obviously they were angry at something or someone beside a group of students with whose opinions they disagreed. And just as obviously, someone in your capitol of Washington was trying to help them give a name to their misfortunes: not Jews, but pacificists, peacenicks, long-hairs and hippies. When my children want to join a parade now, I urge them to try to discover what that parade is *really* all about! . . ."

THE INDIFFERENT ONES

"Every week you pick up a newspaper you have to say: 'My God!' I feel like I'm standing in the surf and just as I am hit by one wave, another comes and hits me until I'm reeling. I feel like drawing myself inward, pulling in my head like a turtle..."

"I never felt so helpless, what can we people at the bottom do? We used to take pride in our vote... I'm thinking of not voting the next time."

"My dad would say: 'All politicians are crooks,' and I used to say 'No.' Now I agree. I feel betrayed."

"I don't keep up with it except on TV, but I kinda feel that if they would leave the President alone, he'd do a better job."

"I'm just as confused as I always was."

—A group of American citizens, interviewed about the Watergate scandal in Portland, Oregon; Milwaukee, Wisconson; Lexington, Kentucky; Beaver Falls, Pennsylvania; and Shaker Heights, Ohio. TIME *November 12, 1973.*

How many times can a man turn his head pretending he just doesn't see?

The answer, my friend, is blowin' in the wind . . .

—"BLOWIN' IN THE WIND"
words and music by Bob Dylan.

"Why do people like you keep asking us what we thought and felt about the Nazis?" asked a handsome blonde woman in a Berlin suburb in 1973. "I was fourteen when Hitler came to power, and I couldn't have cared less. I was never interested in politics . . . all politicians are crooks, yours as well as ours. What does politics have to do with me? I'm a zoologist, and frankly, animals have always interested me more than human beings. I felt that way when I was an adolescent, and I feel that way now."

She also insisted that she did not join the Hitler Youth "because that kind of thing just didn't appeal to me," and that she spent most of her youth in the country, reading, playing the violin and bird watching. "What did you do about the war in Vietnam? You may not have liked all those stories about children being burned by napalm or My Lai, or the bombing of hospitals, but you didn't do much about that, right? And I bet you didn't stay awake nights worrying about the war, did you? Of course, your press informed you a lot better than ours did, and you wouldn't be shot for protesting. But how many Americans really cared about Vietnam or Watergate, or whatever it was you did to blacks and American Indians, for that matter? Very few of you, I bet. You worry about the price of food and getting ahead in your profession, and you probably have some kind of hobby. My hobby is music, not politics. I don't think very many people would list 'honest government' as their prime interest, when they are asked about their concerns on a questionnaire . . . today or any other time. No, I don't feel guilty about what happened in Germany under Hitler. Why should I? Do you feel guilty about Vietnam?"

I told her that I did. She looked surprised. "You must be

the guilty type. Have you thought of seeing a psychiatrist? But then, I don't really believe in psychiatrists either. Most of them are crooks, too."

Hilda said all this in a completely detached, unemotional voice. She told of her childhood and youth, completely divorced from what was going on around her, living in the country and "minding my own business." She had, of course, heard some bombs exploding in the distance; but because of her family's wealth and connections, she lived on an estate so far removed from a major city that not one bomb or shell fell near it. "When the Americans 'liberated' us, they took over our house," she said resentfully. "I told them I didn't believe in killing . . . I wouldn't even step on an ant, so why bother me about something that a bunch of crazy men did, even if it was in my name. I've never voted in an election and I never will. All governments are alike, and I couldn't care less who runs the country as long as I'm left alone."

Hilda's story about not being a member of the Hitler Youth did not check out. She had indeed been a member, but a very inactive one. It would have been impossible for her not to join. If she wished to go to school, membership was almost surely mandatory in her town. But friends remember that she missed most meetings because she was "sick" or because "she couldn't get transportation into the town." "Perhaps she really didn't know or care," one neighbor said. "Unless the whole miserable situation was forced on you, you really often tried to avoid coming to grips with it."

Hilda's mother, an elderly, highly educated widow, presents a different picture. Her best friend had been a Jewish woman, whose first husband, a Socialist, was arrested early in 1936. He died in prison four days later. She remembers going into town to try to console her friend. "Obviously, I was taking a risk going to see her under the circumstances, but we had been close for so long . . ." she said. She also smuggled fresh vegetables, sausages and loaves of bread from their estate to her friend when rations for Jews had reached the starvation level.

"Sometime, in 1940, my friend fell in love and married again. Of course, I couldn't go to the wedding . . . that would have been too dangerous, but I prayed that she'd manage somehow to be happy. Her second husband was taken to a concentration camp six months later. She never heard from him again. She hanged herself in 1941 . . ." The older woman's eyes filled with tears. Had she never discussed any of this with her daughter? "One doesn't want to worry one's children, does one?" she said. "Hilda was so absorbed in her bird watching and her music . . . there was no point in telling her all these sad things. Youth is supposed to be a happy time . . ." It seemed useless and rather cruel to point out that by 1941 Hilda really wasn't all that young anymore.

In a small villa outside of Berlin, lives a German composer whose hit songs were popular not only in Germany, but all over the world. A dapper little man in a red smoking jacket with a white silk scarf, he said that, of course, he "regrets" Germany's past. "But I was an artist, so politics really wasn't my field," he pointed out. "I knew that Hitler liked my music. I had written a children's opera, and he even suggested to Dr. Goebbels [the Minister of Propaganda] that he take his *own* children to see it. Not only that, when young men were drafted into the army, I got a draft exemption because Hitler considered me a fellow artist and felt that my musical compositions would inspire the German nation. Naturally, I was proud of this distinction. Everyone wants to be appreciated, don't they?"

He said that he had remained a civilian, writing songs for "practically every German army unit." "What was expected of me was a lot of trash, of course, but then popular taste isn't what one would like it to be," he added. "The words of the songs were full of hate and referred frequently to enemy blood streaming in rivers down gutters, and enemy cities being bombed into rubble. I thought some of that was really in exceedingly bad taste . . . much overdone. But I didn't write the words, only the music. They had all kinds of official poets in charge of words. That was not my responsibility. As a matter of fact, Dr. Goebbels, himself, wrote the words to one of my melodies." That fact still seemed to fill him with a certain amount of pride. Had he ever been a Nazi? "Well, of course, everybody had to join the party and the party Musicians Association. But I never took any of that very seriously. After all, I'm an artist, not a politician . . ." he repeated.

The same point was made by an outstanding German film producer who was in her late teens and early twenties during the last years of the Weimar Republic and the early Hitler years. "I just pointed my camera and filmed," she said. "I did the best job possible. Many of my techniques are still being copied by people in my field today. Yes, I made propaganda films for the Nazis. That was the only work I could get . . . and work was more important to me than anything else." Looking at her documentaries, which are kept on file in the film archives of the National Archives, it's easy to see that this film maker, unlike the rather ordinary composer, is a true genius in her craft. Therefore, she finds it difficult to understand and accept the fact that many theaters throughout the world won't show her current work, that she has not been employed by either German or U.S. television. "That's where the most important innovations could be made today," she says. "Why do people have to mix art and politics?" she asks rather angrily. "I never did . . ."

A common thread runs through all the interviews with Germans who insist that they didn't know what was happening in their country during the early, or even the late, Hitler years. Most consider politics something that should concern politicians, and possibly government professors, but certainly not themselves. "What can a little man do anyhow?" "After all, I was an artist, a zoologist, a postman, a baker . . . I didn't have any influence . . ." "I never got involved in anything that didn't concern me . . . politics didn't. I took care of my family, isn't that everybody's first responsibility?" "I did what I was told, and didn't ask questions. I thought that the people running the government knew more about their business than I did. Good citizens obey their leaders. I still feel that way. Look at what all those rowdy, rude demonstrators accomplish today. Nothing, except give their country a bad name." These are some of the quotes taken from my tapes in several German cities. Hilda was right, in a way. There are similar quotes on tapes made for other stories about the war in Vietnam, My Lai, police brutality and corruption, Watergate. Only those tapes were recorded in towns and cities in the United States.

THE WHITE ROSE

"Freedom of speech, freedom of religion, protection for each individual citizen against the arbitrary and criminal power of each state . . . those should be the basic principles of the New Europe."

"Support the resistance. Disseminate these pamphlets . . ."

" 'Freedom and Honor' . . . For ten long years Hitler and his cohorts have used these beautiful words that symbolize nothing but disgust, turned them around so that . . . the highest values of our nation have been thrown to the pigs . . ."

"Our people stand in revolt against the enslavement of Europe through the National Socialists, and we are moving towards a new and real meaning of the words 'Freedom and Honor.' "

—*Excerpts from the last two pamphlets published by the student movement "The White Rose" at the University of Munich.*

"Long Live Freedom."

—*The last words of Hans Scholl before he laid his head on the block for the executioner.*

Hans and Sophie Scholl were proud, beautiful and idealistic in 1933. When Hitler came to power, Hans was fifteen, Sophie twelve. In describing their life and death, their sister, Inge, in her book *The White Rose* tells of their first reaction when it was announced in the newpapers and on the radio that Hitler had become chancellor.

"For the first time politics entered our lives," she wrote. "We had heard a great deal about our country, about comradeship, love of our fellow citizens and patriotism. We were very impressed . . . because we loved our country very much, the woods, the river, the gray rocks that rose between the fruit orchards and the vineyards. We could smell the scent of moss, damp earth, and fragrant apples when we thought of our homeland. Of course, 'our country' was only an extension of this landscape we loved, belonging to all of those who spoke the same language and who belonged to the same nation. We loved all of this, although we really couldn't say or understand why. Before, no one had talked to us about this love very much. But now, suddenly, it was as if it were written in great singing letters, in the heavens . . .

"And everywhere, all the time, we heard that Hitler would help our country regain greatness, happiness, pride and prosperity. He would assure everyone of work and food. He would not rest until every single German was a more independent, happier and freer person. We found this a marvelous prospect, and, of course, anything we could do to advance this goal we would do gladly.

"To all of this idealism was added another dimension that attracted us because it seemed almost mystical. We saw the compact, marching units of young people, flags flying, with their bands and their songs. It seemed overwhelming to us . . . this sudden sense of unity and comradeship. So to us it was only natural to join the Hitler Youth, Hans, Sophie . . . all the rest of us.

"We were devoted body and soul to the cause, and we couldn't understand why our father was neither proud nor happy about our decision. He tried to oppose what we wanted to do. Sometimes he said: 'Don't believe them . . . they are wolves and tyrants . . . they are misusing you and the German people.' Occasionally he would compare Hitler to the Pied Piper of Hamelin, the ratcatcher who seduced the children into following him to their doom with the gay tunes of his flute. But our father's words might as well have been spoken into the winds, and his attempts to restrain us were shattered by our youthful enthusiasm."

However, the Scholls, unlike others, had open minds and strong consciences. Their enthusiasm lasted only a few months. Small incidents occurred that in themselves seemed unimportant, but that led to questions for which there were no answers. For instance, Hans was a talented guitar player and folk singer. He had gathered songs from many countries, and he used to sing around the campfires. Soon he was informed that these foreign songs were outlawed: only the songs in the official Hitler song book were acceptable. When he laughed at that seemingly irrational order, he was threatened with punishment. He stopped singing. A book of poems he loved also went on the forbidden list. It was written by a Jew. Another book was banned: the author was a pacificist. Both writers had been forced to flee Germany.

Once the youngest member of his Hitler Youth troop designed and made a flag that in the boy's opinion symbolized all that was great about their country. The troop leader said that the flag would have to be destroyed, only official symbols were allowed. When the youngster refused to give up his prized creation, the troop leader first denounced him furiously, then grabbed the flag and ripped it up. Hans stepped out of his place in the troop and slapped the leader. The tearful face of the young boy whose creation had been dishonored was too much for him to bear. After that, Hans lost his own leadership position in the troop.

Other, more serious incidents came to the Scholls' attention. A favorite teacher disappeared mysteriously. The day before his disapperance, he had been ordered to stand in front of a group of Brownshirts, each of whom, slowly and deliberately, spat in his face. The Scholls asked the teacher's mother what her son had done to deserve such treatment. "Nothing," the desperate woman answered them. "He just wasn't a National Socialist. *That* was his crime."

Rumors about concentration camps began to circulate in the small town of Forchtenberg, of which Herr Scholl, years before, had been mayor. Because the children suspected that he knew more than many others, and because they also felt that he would have the courage to tell them what he knew, they began to ask questions. "This is a kind of war . . ." he told them. "War during peace . . . a battle against our fellow citizens, against the helpless . . . and against the life and freedom of all our children. It is a terrible crime."

He also explained that the decline in unemployment was due to the huge war machine Hitler was building. "It's easy to control unemployment in a dictatorship," he said. "But material security is not enough to give us either happiness or stability. We are first of all human beings, with our own ideas and convictions. A government that tries to tamper with these has no respect for us. And that respect is our most basic human right. I want you to go through life proud and free . . . even if it is difficult."

Herr Scholl's wish would come true. His son and daughter would go through life (what was left of it) proud and free. He also had no inkling of how difficult it was going to be.

At first, Hans and Sophie, and their brothers and sisters, withdrew quietly from their Hitler Youth activities. They spent more and more time within the family, which according to Inge Scholl became a "tight little island." Eventually, they found friends who were as disillusioned as they were, and who also yearned to read the books that were forbidden, to sing the songs that were not approved, to think the thoughts that were not in the official publications. Often they got together to discuss their feelings and ideas. Everyone realized that this was dangerous. Some of their friends were arrested and jailed, usually because someone reported their independent activities. Certainly the local Nazi spies who operated in every village and in every city block must have been suspicious of the group of young people that kept to itself and did not participate in any of the political rallies and meetings that were being called constantly.

But everything went rather well for members of the immediate family, at least. Hans wanted to go to medical school and was accepted at the University of Munich, one of the finest in Germany. Sophie first decided to become a kindergarten teacher and spent two years training for that profession. Then, with the start of World War II, everything changed. Hans and one of his brothers were called into the army, although Hans was eventually sent back to the university to continue his studies. Germany needed physicians. Sophie was called into the State Labor Service and then into the Auxiliary Military Service. But she, too, was released and followed her brother to the University of Munich, where she studied biology and philosophy. Hans saw, during his medical school rounds, wounded soldiers who told in whispers of the massacres of Poles, Russians and Jews. Among the physicians there were rumors that orders had gone out in some hospitals to kill the retarded, the mentally ill, and the handicapped Germans who were not "productive."

Again, the Scholls collected around them a small group of friends. Again, they began to discuss their ideas and feelings. As they became more and more appalled at what was happening around them, they formed a small resistance group called "The White Rose," composed of students and a few teachers to protest their government's actions. They began to publish leaflets, which they printed on an old mimeograph machine, "to strive for the renewal of the mortally wounded German spirit." Sophie transported the leaflets in an old suitcase, and they were sometimes distributed in corridors at the University of Munich; sometimes they were scattered out of windows.

Copies of the White Rose publications found their way to other universities. Each leaflet urged the finder to reprint the message and to pass it on.

Almost miraculously "The White Rose" continued to operate for about a year. However, on February 18, 1943, the inevitable happened. Sophie Scholl and her brother Hans were arrested at the university with a suitcase full of pamphlets. They were sentenced to death by a special, so-called people's court four days later. Also sentenced were Christopher Probst, a young friend of the Scholls, and Professor Kurt Huber, Willi Graf and Alexander Schmorell, all White Rose members. The sentences were carried out within hours of the verdict.

During her brief incarceration before her trial and execution Sophie wrote: "My heart soon gets lost in petty anxieties and forgets that death is near. It is quite unprepared, quickly distracted by frivolous incidentals, it could easily be taken by surprise when the hour comes and miss the one great joy for the sake of little pleasures.

"I realize this, but not so my heart. It continues to dream, refuses to listen to reason, is lulled into safety by the consoling words of irritating wardens, and fluctuates between joy and sorrow. Sorrow is all that is left, paralysis, utter helplessness and a faint hope.

"My heart clings to these treasures, to the promise of a sweet life; tear me away against my will because I am too weak to do it myself. Let me wait till I am miserable and in pain before I dream away salvation."

After their deaths, the Scholls became underground heroes to a great many university students who shared their ideas, but not their willingness to lose their lives.

In an interview a few months ago a high German government official, whose father had been a more cautious member of the German underground and who had thus escaped with his life, said: "When my father heard that the Scholls had been arrested, he mourned: 'If only they had asked me . . . I would have told them to stop their wild and useless rebellion, which inevitably cost them their lives. I would have told them to save themselves for the new Germany that would need people like them desperately, after the war was over.' Now I'm not so sure. We, as Germans, in our overwhelming guilt, need bright, morally untarnished examples like Hans and Sophie Scholl. Their death was a terrible price to pay for the minimum of pride and honor we have left . . . but perhaps it was worth paying."

The terrible price the Scholls and their friends payed for scattering their mimeographed pamphlets out of a university window might not have been necessary, however, if adults in 1933 had been half as wise and as courageous as these young people. It might have been relatively safe (and probably effective) to protest the two-month jail sentence given to the editor of the Essen paper in 1933; it was impossible even to mourn publically the death of the White Rose members in 1943.

DACHAU IS ALSO A TOWN

"One day, sometime in the summer of 1944, my friend Karl Hanke, the Gauleiter of Lower Silesia, came to see me. In earlier years, he had told me a great deal about the Polish and French campaigns, had spoken of the dead and wounded, the pain and agony, and in talking about these things, had shown himself a man of sympathy and directness. This time, sitting in a green leather chair in my office, he seemed confused and spoke falteringly, with many breaks. He advised me never to accept an invitation to inspect a concentration camp. Never, under any circumstances. He had seen something there that he was not permitted to describe and moreover could not describe."

—*Albert Speer*, INSIDE THE THIRD REICH.

Speer was Hitler's Minister of Armaments and Production. A former architect, he was totally devoted to doing his highly technical job well. Those who remember him say that he was not a very political man—more interested in technology than in moral issues. In his book he makes it clear that the first hint he received about the concentration camps was during this conversation with Karl Hanke. And he did as he was advised. He never went to a concentration camp, nor did he discuss the information he had received with anyone; not with personal friends, his colleagues or with Hitler, whom he saw almost every day.

Many Germans will tell an interviewer that they had received hints about concentration camps sometime during the Hitler years. Most will add that they just didn't believe the stories. "After all, the British and Americans circulated those wild tales about German soldiers cutting off babies' hands in Belgium during World War I . . . and those weren't true either," is one of the most frequent answers one gets when one asks how so many Germans maintained their ignorance of the camps, which were usually located on the outskirts of large urban areas.

Not all Germans claim ignorance. "How could we not have known?" one teacher asked. "After all the Nazis didn't exactly keep those camps a secret. I remember reading about the opening of the first camp, Dachau, in an official government publication when I was in high school."

The teacher, of course, is correct. The *Voelkischer Beobachter* of March 21, 1933, carried a press release from "Police Commandant Heinrich Himmler" that a camp for 5,000 people had been opened in Bavaria. According to the news story, the release was prepared because of "countless inquiries" from the public about what had happened to friends and neighbors who had simply disappeared. Incidentally, the story in the next column of the paper says that liberal, left-leaning publications throughout Germany would from that time on no longer be allowed to publish "to preserve public peace and order."

Those living near who were curious and honest enough to trust their five senses could not help knowing about Dachau in any case. "We lived about two city blocks from the camp gates," a waiter in a small Bavarian restaurant said. "There was no way for any resident of the area to escape the fact that Dachau existed and that, for many, it was a death camp. When I was thirteen, I remember coming home late one night from a hiking trip with my Hitler Youth Group and meeting, on the public road, a cart filled to overflowing with dead bodies. We all got sick. Our troop leader quickly led us down a side road. How can you hide almost 32,000 deaths, occuring right on your doorstep? After all, Dachau wasn't just a camp . . . it was also a town."

"You could smell the camp blocks away," another lifelong resident of the town, a pleasant middle-class suburb of Munich, said. "Sometimes at night you would hear screams. You heard the barking of the vicious guard dogs. And although the dead were always carted away in the early predawn hours, there were people on the road when the carts and trucks rolled by. Perhaps those of us who knew the most asked the fewest questions. By March of 1933, we already knew that asking questions could be very unhealthy. Our parents, our teachers, every adult we respected, told us that. No one who lived and worked near that camp needed an explanation of exactly what was meant by 'unhealthy.' "

Dachau was the first of the concentration camps. It was originally meant for known Communists and Socialists, intellectuals who disagreed with the government in power, journalists who continued to publish stories unfavorable to the government even when warned that this was not in the national interest, and others whom the party in power considered to be dangerous to the unity and order of the new Germany. From the beginning, conditions were more unbearable at the camp than in Germany's worst prisons, where murderers, thieves and other criminals were incarcerated. Certainly, if a murderer in an ordinary prison died under suspicious circumstances, there was an official investigation. Thousands died in Dachau, and as far as anyone can recall, there were never any questions, except possibly from the victim's family and friends. And even they learned quickly that many questions might be "unhealthy."

In a way, the German government never meant to keep the camps for political prisoners a secret. The camps were part of the terror tactics used to make sure that everybody stayed in line.

German officials also wanted to keep a certain mystery around the camps, because what's mysterious is frequently more terrifying. In the early years, some prisoners were released after months or years in the camps. Before their release, they signed a paper promising that they would discuss with no one what had happened to them there. "My father reappeared with a shaved head, frightened eyes and a gaunt, starved face about a year after he was arrested," one educator, now a member of the German parliament, said. "He had screaming nightmares till the day of his death, three years after his release. Cause of death was diagnosed as kidney failure. There had never been anything wrong with my father's kidneys before his arrest. One family doctor told us that the kidney damage was probably the result of beatings he had received at the camp. 'But, at least, he had a few good years at home,' he told my mother consolingly. I'm not at all sure how good those years were."

Dachau is now a museum, with one of the original long, low barracks and its three-tiered rows of bunks reconstructed for visitors. The museum also contains wall panels with pictures taken by guards during the Nazi years and by American journalists and army photographers after the town and camp were occupied by American troops at the end of the war. More shocking than even the most graphic pictures of starving, suffering, brutalized human beings of all ages are the copies of typewritten, itemized, carefully legalistic orders and documents giving specific instructions on how, when and under what circumstances, prisoners (both men and women) were to be flogged or otherwise tortured. The orders mention the thickness of the clubs to be used, the height of the table on which the victims were to be stretched out, and the fact that they were to be hit on naked parts of their bodies.

Another order specifies that "for the good of humanity," prisoners could be subjected to "medical experiments." The document is on the same wall panel as the picture of an eighteen-year-old man who died in a pressure chamber experiment.

Another letter ordered that "for humanitarian reasons . . . women condemned to death have no knowledge of the impending execution."

Many of these orders were mimeographed. It is impossible to believe that they were seen by only one or two people. Like everything else in Nazi Germany, these orders were obviously processed through a long line of command.

The residents of Dachau often point out that the camp in their town was "not a death camp." "It was a punishment camp," one middle-aged policeman said. "Death camps had gas chambers and crematoria in which bodies could be burned quickly. You don't see anything like that around here." And one doesn't. Only the foundations of the long, stark barracks, which had to be burned down by the American troops, since by the time the camp was liberated, typhoid, dysentery and other epidemics were out of control.

The barracks used as part of the museum was reconstructed by the American Army and used for a while as a military prison for GIs who had gone AWOL, or committed some other military offense. The people of Dachau were puzzled by this action. The widow of a German journalist who had died there said in a rather confused tone: "It somehow seemed like a rather insensitive thing for the Americans to do. We asked them to put their military prisoners somewhere else, but they didn't seem to understand why we objected." Finally, the German government officially requested the American army to "Allow the use of the Dachau campsite as a memorial to the victims who died there," and to remove those delinquent American GIs to other quarters. At that point the army closed out its Dachau branch and the site was turned over entirely to the Bavarian government, which opened the museum on May 9, 1965.

Busloads of tourists visit the site. Often they are high-school classes, Scout troops, young people from many European countries. According to the museum director, few Germans visit.

The man who had seen the death cart on his night hike as

a teenager has never been to the camp. "It still terrifies me," he says. The educator whose father died of kidney disease has not been there either. "I was twelve years old when Dachau opened," he said. "My own father died as a result of what happened to him there. Yet for years I felt so guilty about what had happened in my country, I couldn't even discuss the concentration camps with anyone. So many other terrible things, like Vietnam, have happened since then, that I feel the burden of guilt not quite as strongly anymore. Perhaps it helps to know that Germans were not the only monsters in human history . . . but Vietnam or not, the concentration and extermination camps were unique."

Dachau is also a town, and as in any town there are many opinions on any subject one cares to mention. For instance, there are residents who insist that the stories of the atrocities committed in the camps were exaggerated. "We didn't really kill 6 million Jews," one railroad engineer said, "probably 600,000 is more like it. Americans always exaggerate everything." A woman, who worked as a restaurant cashier, and whose place of business had been robbed recently, thought that "it was about time we stopped glorifying all those prisoners. Half of them were probably criminals anyhow. Places like Dachau made our streets safe at night. Did you know that Germany had the lowest crime rate in its history under Hitler?" A customer who identified herself as the daughter of a Dachau victim looked at her in total disbelief: "Exactly what do you call a crime?" she asked.

THE SURVIVORS

"Holocaust n. (Gr. *holos*, whole + *kaustos*, burnt) 1) complete destruction of people or animals 2) great destruction."

—*Webster's New World Dictionary of*
the American Language.

"A thousand years will pass and the guilt of Germany will not be erased."

—*Hans Frank, Governor General of Poland, before he was*
hanged after the Nuremberg trials as a war criminal.

On one of Berlin's main squares stands a 6-foot memorial to the victims of the Third Reich. It was built from the rubble of the city's main synagogue. Nearby stands a gray, simple modern building with pieces of an ornate doorway and one pillar from the old temple incorporated as part of the architecture. Looking at what remains of the house of worship she remembers from her early childhood, a middle-aged woman whom we shall call Rosa, says bitterly: "Those buildings are survivors, like me . . . small parts of a life we loved but can hardly remember, stuck together with plaster."

Rosa works in the gray modern building, which serves as both temple and a community center for the about 5,000 Jews living today in West Berlin. There used to be almost 200,000. Some lucky ones (like me, for instance) managed to emigrate with or without their families before the holocaust struck. Over 50,000 perished in Hitler's gas chambers. About 1,400 survived the war years in Berlin, largely with the help of a few non-Jewish Germans who hid them, fed them, and kept them from being caught in the almost inescapable Nazi net. No one has been able to account accurately for the rest of Berlin's once thriving and productive Jewish population.

More than 6 million Jews were deliberately murdered in Hitler's Germany. When one thinks in terms of millions or even thousands or hundreds, terror, suffering and death somehow seem impersonal. But what happened will never seem impersonal to Rosa, although she is one of the few still living.

She owes the fact that she is not one of the appalling statistics, but a living, breathing human being, to her mother's religion. Only her father was a Jew; her mother was a Protestant. Rosa and her sister were brought up as Jews, however. Her father felt very strongly about his religious and cultural heritage, and her mother deferred to him. "She must have loved him very much," Rosa says today. "After Hitler, the pressures on her to divorce him were unbelievable. She was promised a good job, extra food, complete protection from any kind of persecution if she would just consent to leave him and us. The alternative to not leaving was probably death, either by slow starvation or in a concentration camp. She chose to stay."

Her father had been a dentist, working in a clinic at a small salary, rather than establishing a well-paid private practice. Because there never was much money, her mother worked as a secretary. Rosa wanted to study dentistry, too. She remembers her father's pride in his work. "Healthy teeth can mean a longer, healthier life," he used to tell her. "Most of my patients would not have a tooth in their mouths by the time they are forty if it weren't for the clinic. They couldn't afford to go to a private dentist." He did not mention the fact that almost none of these patients were Jewish. The neighborhood in which Rosa's family lived and where the clinic was located consisted of large, dingy, six-story tenements. Most of their neighbors were factory workers.

In the early 1930s there weren't many Nazis. Rosa had the impression that in one apartment down the block regular Communist meetings took place once or twice a week. Many of the men in the neighborhood were intensely involved in union activities. When there were strikes and layoffs, they cursed the government. Rosa knew that her parents often lent money or gave food to families with out-of-work fathers. Although he was a dentist and not a family doctor, her father was also often called out in the middle of the night if someone nearby got very ill and no other physician could be persuaded to make a house call. "He kept telling people that he could only administer first aid and try to get the patient into a hospital," she remembers. "Finally he got some of the men and women in the neighborhood together and started an informal first-aid class: what to do if a child was cut or burned, if someone seemed to have a broken bone, if a baby was born prematurely (this happened a lot in our area). Ironically, long after my father had been taken off to a concentration camp, the people used the skills he had taught them to save lives during and after air raids. Occasionally now, I meet someone on the street who tells me that his own life or that of a family member was saved because of the knowledge they had gained at those meetings my father ran."

Rosa had always played with the children in the neighborhood. The only difference between herself and her playmates seemed to be that she went to synagogue on Friday evenings and they went to church on Sundays. Her first encounter with the Nazi movement occurred when she was nine, in 1930. Her best friend lived right across the hall. They had always considered each other's homes almost interchangeable. One day when she rang the friend's doorbell, the girl's mother appeared, physically blocking the apartment's entrance. "I think it would be better if you didn't come here anymore," she told Rosa, who couldn't believe her ears. She remembers hearing her friend, Minna, sobbing somewhere in a back room.

When Rosa, herself in tears, told her mother what had happened, the tired worried woman said: "I have been expecting something like this. Frau Schmidt joined the Nazi party a few months ago . . . and after all, you're a Jew. Perhaps it would be better if you found Jewish friends. Have some of the girls in your synagogue class over for the afternoon. You should get to know them better."

Rosa thought that the whole conversation was sad and peculiar. As far as she knew, she had been Jewish all her life, and she had been friends with Minna almost as long. So what was the problem? She tried to ask Minna, whom she still met in the school playground, and Minna was just as confused and unhappy. "My mother just thinks your family is bad for me," she reported. "She says I'll be punished if I go to your house or let you come to mine when she's not around. There's nothing I can do to change her mind." For a while the two girls continued to meet secretly in the park, in the school yard and in other neutral territory. They passed notes to each other in class. But, inevitably, the friendship cooled.

As the months passed, Minna's apartment was not the only one in which Rosa was no longer welcome. Fewer and fewer of her neighbors and classmates seemed to want to associate with her. She heard her parents discuss the possibility of moving to a "more Jewish" neighborhood, and then agreeing sadly that they couldn't afford to move. It seemed as if her parents, as well as Rosa and her sister, had become completely isolated in a neighborhood in which they had formerly been warmly accepted and regarded by many as leaders.

A year later, Rosa was no longer welcome even in her aunt's house. She had overheard a fierce fight between her mother and her mother's sister in which the sister insisted that the mother leave her husband. "If you have the children baptized immediately, perhaps people will forget that they are half-

Jews. Of course, you'll have to take your maiden name back, and perhaps my husband, who has some influence with a local judge, can arrange to have the girls' name changed legally, too," she said. "Then, of course, you'll have to move to some other town so that nobody will know how you have disgraced yourself."

Rosa also remembers that her usually gentle mother completely lost control of her temper and threw her sister out. The sister ran down the three flights of stairs screaming: "You'll regret that you didn't listen. You've not only hurt yourself and your children, you may have managed to get me and my husband in trouble with the government." Rosa never saw that aunt again. She knows that years later when her father was dead, and she, her sister and her mother were getting the tiny rations of food that were available to half-Jewish Berliners during the late war years, her mother went to the same sister, whose husband was now a Nazi party official, to ask for a little extra food. Rosa had been doing forced labor in a factory (by then she was seventeen) and had become ill with overwork and malnutrition. The aunt closed the door in her mother's face.

The treatment Rosa received during the very early Nazi years from the people in the community that her father had served so faithfully and from her mother's family would have been enough to make anyone bitter. But it was only the beginning. Hers is a typical "survivor" story, with anger growing into despair, fear into terror, and finally, almost into indifference.

In 1933 she first saw the sign *Juden unerwuenscht* (JEWS NOT WELCOME) at movie houses, at the public swimming pool she had used for years, finally even on park benches. The signs disappeared briefly in 1936, when they were quietly removed for the Olympic games, which were held in Germany that year. "We told a few American and English tourists about our life here and about the fact that the signs had been taken down only for their benefit, but I don't think anybody believed us,"

Rosa said. "We stopped talking to foreigners because many of them made it clear that they thought Germany was marvelous . . . clean streets, trains running on time, very little crime, polite smiles everywhere. What was the use of endangering our own lives trying to get these people to see the truth?"

After the Olympics, signs like JEWS NOT ADMITTED or JEWS ENTER AT THEIR OWN PERIL appeared on the doors of pharmacies, grocery stores and bakeries. Rosa often had to walk twenty blocks before she found a store that didn't carry such a sign just to buy a loaf of bread. "At first, I didn't go into any place that let me know I wasn't wanted. I still had some pride left," she said. "But later, I couldn't afford pride anymore. If we needed food or medicine, I'd go into any store that didn't know me. After all, there was no way to tell that I was Jewish." During these years her mother, who, of course, was not a Jew, would probably have been served in neighborhood stores, but she frequently was too sick to shop.

In 1934 her father had been dismissed by the clinic. He opened a small office in the apartment, and many of his former patients still came to him secretly. Eventually one was arrested. After that, he saw only Jewish patients. "He was never quite sure whether or not that man had been arrested only because he went to a Jewish dentist," Rosa recalled. "That man wasn't political, and we couldn't think of any other reason why he would have been suspected. So my father was afraid to let any of his other patients take any chances."

In 1935 the so-called Nuremberg Laws, depriving German Jews of citizenship, were passed. They also forbade marriage between Jews and "Aryans." "We were terrified that the next set of laws would force my mother to leave my father," Rosa said. "That never happened, but in 1938 my father was arrested. Men with fierce dogs appeared at our door in the middle of the night and took him away. He never came back." After a few weeks Rosa's mother learned that she was a widow; she received her late husband's ashes in a cigar box. There was never any explanation for his arrest. Jews were not yet being rounded up indiscriminately, as they would be a few years later. But, apparently, one of the Nazi block wardens had reported that in 1930 her father had attended Communist meetings. That suspicion (unjustified) plus the fact that he was a Jew led to his execution.

A few days later the block warden came to the apartment. If Rosa's mother (who by now was seriously ill with tuberculosis and could get no medical care) would agree to give up custody of her two daughters (they would be sent to a labor camp), she could be reestablished as a full "Aryan," with all her former privileges. She would be allowed to go to a hospital where she might be cured. She might even be eligible for some kind of state pension. "By that time my mother was too sick to throw anybody out, as she had done when her sister asked her to leave us," Rosa said with sad pride. "If she had had the strength, she would have."

There was less and less money, and the family finally took in a boarder, a retired Jewish schoolteacher, who after forty years as a civil servant, had lost her state pension. She was living on her savings. "They'll probably last as long as I will," she said frequently.

Since all "Aryan" places of public education and entertainment were closed to them, Rosa and her sister came to count more and more on the synagogue and the Jewish Community Center for relief from their daily drudgery at a factory making army uniforms and their constant worry about money and food. "The Community Center had marvelous plays and operas. Outstanding Jewish musicians who were not allowed to perform anywhere else in Germany and who had not left the country performed there," Rosa recalled. "With all our problems, we were grateful to our father for bringing us up in his religion. If we had become Protestants, the German government would have given us the same label, *Mischling* (someone of mixed blood), that they gave us anyhow, and we would have had no one and nothing with which we could identify."

But by the end of 1938 their social center was gone, too.

In an orgy of burning, looting and window breaking that became known as *Kristallnacht* (night of glass), storm troopers destroyed Jewish-owned businesses, homes, hospitals, schools—and the main synagogue and community center. Both were smashed into the rubble that is now incorporated into the memorial and the new Jewish Center.

Rosa read about the destruction in the newspaper. Apparently, a German consular officer had been attacked by a French student in Paris. The student was presumed to have been Jewish, and, according to official reasoning, "an outraged German people was taking its revenge on the guilty Jews." Nobody explained why all those "outraged" Germans were storm troopers, why the police stood quietly by watching the looting of stores and the desecration of temples. And why, for that matter, the whole demonstration was confined mainly to Berlin. Weren't the Germans in the other German towns and cities equally indignant? Or was it in Berlin alone some semblance of Jewish community spirit had been kept alive? A few businesses had still flourished, keeping many Jews employed. The cultural life that Rosa enjoyed so much had received a considerable amount of underground attention. Berliners, accustomed to some of the best theater, art and music in the world, did not patronize the "approved" German art shows and plays. With many of its top musicians and conductors gone, the once world-renowned Berlin Philharmonic seemed like a caricature of its old self. And some non-Jewish Germans had actually said that they wished they could attend some of the theatrical and musical performances at the Jewish Community Center. Now the center and the synagogue were destroyed, and the "threat" of Jewish artistic and cultural life along with it.

The following Friday Rosa went to see what was left of the synagogue. She saw a pile of rubble, but she also saw one thing that made her shudder even more. Old Jewish men and women who had tried to salvage some of the holy objects that might have remained after the fire were cleaning the street on their hands and knees with toothbrushes under the clubs and whips of Nazi storm troopers. "We'll show those arrogant bastards a thing or two," one strong, handsome, bright-eyed young man said loudly. "We told them to stay out of that building. They will learn to obey our orders." Rosa remembers that a few bystanders applauded, but that many looked deeply embarrassed and backed away from the scene as inconspicuously as they could. Nor was such an open and public humiliation of elderly Jews ever repeated in Berlin. Apparently no one would stop it (it might have cost the protester's life or at least his or her freedom). But it must have been obvious to the authorities that there was no spontaneous outburst of approval either.

After the beginning of World War II, laws were passed that said all Jews had to wear a yellow star on their clothing at all times, not just in Germany but in all the countries Germany had occupied. Rumors appeared in the German-Jewish community that the King of Denmark had appeared with a yellow star on his arm the first morning the order went into effect in his country. That rumor turned out to be true. Jews were rounded up on the streets and in their homes. They were told that they were going to labor camps, but none ever returned. One day the police came for the teacher who boarded in Rosa's apartment. "Well, I said that I'd last about as long as my savings," she sighed. "It looks as if my bank account has lasted longer than me. I'm not coming back. You keep the money." She was never heard from again.

Rosa and her sister now were stopped and questioned regularly in the street and at work. Once, when Rosa came home she found a secret police team questioning her mother. She had forgotten to pin on her yellow star that morning, and when she entered the apartment, she was terrified. She knew that failure to wear the star could mean prison. She and her sister were indeed taken away to police headquarters over the anguished protests of her terrified, sick mother. They spent the night there, and in the morning, without explanation, they were allowed to go home.

Much later, after Berlin was occupied by the Allied troops,

she learned that an order had gone out to round up *Mischlinge* as well as other Jews for transportation to a concentration camp and death. But the authorities had found that they could not provide the necessary cattle cars, and that the gas chambers in the camps were already working overtime and running out of the cyanide gas used to kill the victims. The order was reversed: *Mischlinge* who could work in defense industries were to be left in their homes. Their turn would come later. "We know that if the war had lasted another six months, we also would have been dead," Rosa said. "Thank God it didn't."

So Rosa and her sister were among the 1,400 survivors when American and Russian troops took over the city. For the last few weeks they hid in cellars to escape the bombs and the still eager Nazi persecutors who were shooting men, women and children with yellow stars on sight. At American military headquarters, Jews were asked to identify themselves, to get ration cards, priority on available jobs and temporary housing if that was needed. Rosa's mother lived just long enough to see her daughters safe. She died three days after American troops took over the district.

"When we came out of hiding, we realized for the first time how few of our friends had survived," Rosa said. "There was almost no one left. The Americans took good care of us, and perhaps we should have been happy that we were among the few still left alive and relatively healthy. But we were all deeply depressed. We gorged ourselves on the food that was given us . . . and then we got sick. We couldn't sleep; many of us cried almost all the time. One of us, a young man who had studied psychology in the pre-Nazi days, told us we were suffering all the symptoms of extreme guilt. But why were we so guilty? We hadn't done anything or betrayed anybody. He told us that we felt that way because we were survivors. Why had we been singled out to escape the holocaust, when so many other innocent men, women and children were dead?"

Rosa has never been able to overcome the guilt or the bitterness. It has shadowed her whole life. She never married. "I couldn't let myself get close to anyone. All the people I had loved when I was a child had died. I didn't want to feel that kind of anguish again . . . so I didn't allow myself to feel much love either," she said. Many other survivors echo her feelings. Another *Mischling* who had survived because only his mother was a Jew talks about his five marriages and five divorces. "Every time I really allowed myself to love someone, I had to run," he said. "You can't live in constant fear for one-third of your life, and then return to a normal existence. I can't really trust anyone . . . ever. I can't have children because I'd be too terrified about what would happen to them. I can't really live the way a normal person can." He didn't sound self-pitying when he made his statement, just matter of fact.

Rosa works with old people at the Jewish Community Center now. Many of these people emigrated to the United States or other countries before the extermination squads came to Berlin. They never felt at home in their adopted homes so they returned after the war. But the only place in which they feel totally comfortable is in that Center. They come there early in the morning, stay for reading, discussion groups, card playing, religious services and meals. It's also the only place where Rosa feels comfortable. "Some of my old neighbors have come to me to 'apologize' for what happened. How can you apologize for 6 million deaths?" she says. "Everybody assures me that they didn't know about the extermination camps. I don't believe them. After all, *I* knew about them . . . why should I be so much better informed than my Aryan neighbors? We read the same papers; we heard the same broadcasts. We all knew that people disappeared and were never heard from again. What did *they* think was happening to all those Jews? They didn't think at all. It was easier that way."

What would she have done if she had been one of the Aryans? Would she have protested, or tried to save a Jewish neighbor? "I don't know," she says. "I can't imagine how I would have acted. A few Germans sacrificed their lives for some of us; would I have been one of them? Who can really know about themselves? But I do know that our fellow citizens, people we thought were our friends, stood by silently while we were swallowed up by the gas chambers and crematoria. That's impossible to understand, and even more impossible to forgive." Her eyes are wet, but her voice is hard. She turns to help an old man crippled with arthritis sit down in a lounge chair. "How are things for you today, Herr Cohen?" she asks. "About as usual," says the old man. "But what can you expect ... after all, I'm alive, aren't I?"

WHERE WAS
EVERYBODY ELSE?

"Across the bridge . . . returning from an outing, marches a group of small boys, wearing the uniform of the Hitler Youth . . . short black trousers, brown shirts, and a handkerchief slipped through a braided leather holder. They are singing in an accurately pitched, youthful treble that moving, modern national song: 'The Horst Wessel Lied.' "

—*Douglas Chandler*, NATIONAL GEOGRAPHIC, *February 1937.*

A German journalist, about my age, handed me a worn and yellowed copy of the *National Geographic* of February 1937. His gesture was a direct answer to the question I had asked him and many others: "Didn't anybody in Germany see what was happening? Why did so few people try to stop Hitler, in the early years, when it still might have been possible?" He answered my question with one of his own: "Why do you *just* ask Germans? Where was everybody else? Certainly foreign diplomats and journalists had an opportunity to see what was happening. Well, here's a good description of what some *thought* they saw."

The feature article in that 1937 American magazine was called "The Life and Luster of Berlin," written by a well known free-lance reporter from Baltimore, Douglas Chandler.

Besides the Chandler text, there were twenty-four color photographs (among the first color pages that *National Geographic* had ever published) taken, according to an explanatory note, by "several editors of the magazine." Apparently not just Mr. Chandler but several other magazine staffers had visited Germany to do that story.

"I kept this copy of *National Geographic*, because it's the last issue I ever saw until long after World War II," the German journalist explained. "My father canceled our subscription. 'If I want to read Nazi propaganda I can get it free of charge,' he said. 'I don't have to send all the way to the United States for it.'" The journalist's father was well known in his own circle for his strongly anti-Nazi sentiments. He was jailed briefly a few times, but was kept out of a concentration camp because he was a prominent and highly placed Protestant layman with influential friends. He had subscribed to *National Geographic* for his children, to give them a picture of the world outside of Germany—of the geography, botany, customs and ideas of other lands from Africa to the Arctic. He knew that a subscription to a foreign magazine made you suspect with the government because the German postal service reported all such subscribers. "It hardly seems worthwhile taking a chance for a publication that's more enthusiastic about the Nazis than many German publications," he told his son, who had loved the magazine and was angry about the cancellation.

It did seem to me after reading the last paragraph of the *National Geographic* article that I was looking at a satire. The piece was published in 1937. The Nazis had been in power for about four years, and thousands of Germans had already been murdered. The "moving, modern, national song," the Horst Wessel Lied, urged German youth on to revenge and bloody battle against a vast variety of imagined foes. But my German colleague urged me to read the whole article, from beginning to end, including the captions under those striking color photographs. "You can believe me that guy Chandler wasn't kidding . . . and neither were the editors who printed the piece. I might remind you that our newspapers were forced to print this kind of garbage . . . yours were not."

It turned out that Mr. Chandler was, indeed, overflowing with admiration. He wasn't just thrilled with the new German music, but with Berlin's urban renewal. "I walked the streets of the Old City and found myself humming the line of the Princeton Triangle Club song . . . 'Renovate, rejuvenate, and change the date,' " he wrote. The Old City had indeed been renovated. It had been filled with Jewish-owned shops whose owners had been dispossessed. The storefronts were being "rejuvenated" to make room for the new Nazi owners, who had taken over without bothering with such formalities as payment. Even the line about the change in date was essentially correct, although not exactly in the way that Chandler indicated. Germany had, for about 150 years, been a hospitable place for Jews fleeing persecution in Eastern Europe. Berlin especially had become a center for the best of Jewish culture, science, and tradition, as well as for commerce and industry. Now Germany was going right back to the attitudes of the Middle Ages. Most Berliners, including teenagers, were only too aware of this. Apparently, one of America's most respected magazines was not.

Chandler was also almost ecstatic about the new Youth Movement. "To develop boys and girls in body and mind to insure a sturdy race to defend Germany in the future is the policy of the German government," he wrote in describing the Hitler Youth activities. He didn't ask, "Defend against whom?" nor, apparently, did his editors. He did point out that the Boy and Girl Scout movement had been banned in Germany, but he insisted that the Hitler Youth was a more than adequate substitute "enormously popular with all classes." He forgot to mention that membership in the Nazi Youth organization was not voluntary. If he had asked our own next-door neighbors, for instance, he would have learned that the father of the family was jailed for refusing to let his children join and that the youngsters were expelled from school. Eventually, they had to sign up anyhow; their parents' lives might have been in danger had the refusal continued.

Chandler noted that "flowers fill a role of high spiritual importance in the lives of the new Berliners." He indicated in his article that he had often visited Germany and Berlin before. Was it possible that he had not noticed that now the benches in the flower-filled parks (old Berliners had also loved greenery) now bore signs that said: JEWS ARE NOT PERMITTED TO SIT HERE?

Indeed Chandler's only mention of the Jewish problem is contained in one sentence: "A law passed several years ago requires that electrocution be employed as the method of killing animals in slaughterhouses. Kosher killing is strictly prohibited." The flower-loving Nazis were so fond of animals that they insisted that pigs, geese and cows be slaughtered as mercifully as possible, while human beings were being starved and beaten to death in German prisons and camps. There is no mention of political repression in the article.

"I wonder how many cancellations National Geographic received from American readers after they published that piece?" the German journalist asked. "Could you find out for me? I'd really be interested. It might be a partial answer, at least to my question: 'Where was everybody else?'"

A check with National Geographic revealed very little. Apparently there had not been a wave of indignation after the article appeared, nor very many canceled subscriptions. What had happened was that the Baltimore journalist, Douglas Chandler, had allowed his enthusiasm for the Nazi system to overcome him to the point of remaining in Germany and making a number of overseas broadcasts under the pseudonym "Paul Revere" to the United States during World War II. He returned to this country after the war and was convicted of treason. He was later pardoned. Obviously, he was not an objective reporter. If he had been the only American to endorse the Nazi system in a respectable publication, the whole incident of the article might be regarded as a one-time freak—

poor reporting on the part of one writer, and bad journalistic judgment on the part of the editors who printed the piece.

But Chandler's was not the only voice raised in praise of the Nazi system. On the floor of the United States Senate and the House of Representatives, speeches were made to defend Germany's actions and to blame those who opposed them as "Jew lovers" and "warmongers." Out of Detroit, a Catholic priest, Father William Coughlin, was spewing anti-Semitic and pro-Hitler propaganda over the air waves. He was financed by thousands of small contributions from listeners, and (according to reports in some Detroit papers) by large ones from several American industrialists, who disliked the American President, Franklin Delano Roosevelt, a great deal more than they did the German Führer, Adolf Hitler.

In 1940, a book by a sensitive and intelligent American writer, Anne Morrow Lindbergh, became an instant best seller. It was a short essay—*The Wave of the Future: A Confession of Faith*—only forty-one pages long. Its influence on well-meaning Americans was tremendous. *The Reader's Digest* picked it up as its lead story in November of 1940. Anne Lindbergh, the wife of Charles Lindbergh and the daughter of American diplomat William Morrow, had visited Germany several times. She had seen at least some of the evils Chandler had totally ignored. Indeed, she confessed to being "the victim of corroding uneasiness, doubts and fears these past years." In her book she tries to share her feelings with those who "like myself, are not specialists in history, economics or foreign affairs, but who feel that the issues confronting us today are not the concern only of specialists, but equally, the concern of the average citizen."

Actually, she asks more questions than she answers, but her questions all point in one inevitable direction: "Much that is happening in Hitler's Germany is bad . . . but perhaps it will lead to some ultimate good. We, as Americans, do not have the moral right to judge what is happening. After all, we are not perfect ourselves."

"What was pushing behind Communism?" she asked (at

that time Germany and Russia were still allies). "What's behind fascism in Italy? What's behind nazism? Is it nothing but a return to 'barbarism' to be crushed at all costs by a 'crusade'? Or is it some new and perhaps ultimately good conception of humanity trying to come to birth, often through evil and horrible forms?"

She answers her own question in a rather vague, but seductively gentle way: "Something one feels is pushing up through the crust of custom. One does not know what . . . some new conception of humanity and its place on earth. I believe that it is, in its essence, good, but that because we are blind we cannot see it, and because we are too slow to change, it must force its way through the heavy crust violently . . . in eruptions."

Mrs. Lindbergh's book obviously became as successful as it did because she echoed the thoughts of a great many of her fellow countrymen and women. It is no longer available in any library I went to, and has been out of print for almost twenty-five years. But a great many educated Germans quoted passages of that book to me or showed me a copy when I asked them about their Nazi past. "If Anne Lindbergh believed as she did, wrote about it in a free country, had her thoughts and ideas picked up by a magazine with one of the highest circulation figures in the world, how can you blame any of us, with a controlled press, living under a dictatorship, from believing the same things?" one teacher in a small German town asked me. "Of course, I never read that book until after the war, but it echoed my own feelings and ideas exactly. I knew there were things wrong here in 1940, but felt that perhaps out of great wrongs could come great rights."

Of course, the majority of American reporters did not deal in Nazi propaganda, nor allow themselves to be blinded by either vague generalities about the nature of evil or by the "life and luster" of Berlin. They reported what they saw and heard: a rising tide of horror and atrocity with no redeeming social value. However, those reporters worked mainly for newspapers on the East coast and for the major radio networks. The term "Eastern Establishment Press" did not originate with former Vice-President Spiro Agnew. It was applied liberally to the *New York Times,* the *New York Post,* CBS and NBC News, and to reporters like Dorothy Thompson, William L. Shirer, Elmer Davis and Edward R. Murrow, who early recognized the Nazi system for the monstrosity it really was.

Those Germans who believed that no one else cared were wrong. But during those pre-World War II years pro-Nazi or just plain indifferent Americans often told me and those like me who had managed to escape Germany that the ownership of the *New York Times* was Jewish. For every quote from the *Times* that a German refugee could find to prove his or her case against the Nazis, someone could find another quote from a newspaper like the *Chicago Tribune* that contradicted what the *Times* said.

When Hitler first came to power, there were influential men and women, not only in the United States but in Great Britain and France, who felt that Hitler was exactly what Europe needed to fight the Communist menace. When Hitler and Stalin signed their peace pact, the world Communist press was suddenly on the Nazi side as well. The extreme right and the extreme left had brought down the Weimar Republic. The extreme right and the extreme left in other countries united to keep the truth cloudy in the minds of many Europeans and Americans until it was too late. American and British soldiers who liberated the concentration camps saw, with genuine horror and surprise, the tortured bodies and starved faces of the few survivors, the mountains of old shoes that had belonged to murdered children, the heaps of gold fillings that had been extracted from the teeth of dead victims. They could not understand how all of this could have happened without everyone in Germany rising up and throwing the criminal government out.

What many of these young soldiers did not know was that in the late 1930s, when it was still possible for Jews and other future concentration camp victims to get out of Germany, there was not a country in the world that would allow them to emigrate unconditionally. In the United States a refugee was expected either to have enough money (as my father did) to assure the authorities that he and his family would not become an expense to the American taxpayer or to have friends who would "guarantee" his support with their own funds. In addition, there were immigration quotas.

Other countries were not even that generous. Swiss border patrols were instructed to turn back desperate refugees on mountain passes and to chase them to certain death in the arms of the Gestapo patrol on the other side. One woman, now married to an American businessman, managed to cross into Switzerland over a mountain pass, and hid in the home of a friend who had been a Swiss exchange student in Germany. When she was found by the Swiss police, there was serious talk of sending her back to Germany. Her pleas that she would be shot (she was then fourteen years old) were regarded as the ravings of a hysterical child. She was allowed to remain only because war broke out between Germany and France, and the technicalities of returning her were considered too complicated.

Switzerland was, of course, not the only country that did not wish to play host to desperate refugees from Nazi terror. One of the most tragic incidents occurred as late as May 13, 1939, just before the beginning of World War II. A German ship, the *St. Louis*, sailed from Hamburg with 937 Jews and other endangered people on board. They had been allowed to buy their way out of Germany and had purchased visas for Cuba. Most hoped, eventually, to be allowed to come to the United States. They had quota numbers for immigration to this country, but they knew that these numbers were too high, and that by the time their permits would be issued, they would long since have been killed by the Nazis.

Before the ship was halfway across the Atlantic, a power struggle started between the corrupt Cuban immigration minister, who had issued the visas, and the straitlaced president of that country. The ship, in blistering heat and with little food and water aboard, floundered off the coast of Cuba from May 27 to June 6, while negotiations were conducted between the Joint Distribution Committee, a Jewish international charitable organization, and various governments, none of which was willing to accept the refugees. President Franklin Delano Roosevelt was among those who were approached and asked to pass an executive order to allow the *St. Louis* to dock in Miami, and to grant its human cargo refugee status.

Pressure from right-wing congressmen (who did not wish to see America become involved in an international incident), some labor unions (who worried about high unemployment in America and who feared wholesale immigration from Europe) and others persuaded him to turn down the request. The 937 refugees were told that they would be returned to Germany. Meanwhile, Propaganda Minister Goebbels boasted in the German press that "we are not the only ones who don't want this Jewish scum." He also indicated that if the people who had fled from Germany landed in Hamburg, they would be taken immediately to extermination camps.

On the ship, families became increasingly more terrified. The ship's physician ran out of sedatives, which were used to keep the desperate people from hurling themselves over the side of the ship. Nevertheless, there were several suicide attempts. Suicide patrols were established to keep a close watch on men and women who had already served time in concentration camps, and who vowed that they would die, rather than go back.

On Wednesday, June 8, all negotiations with Cuba, the United States, and finally, the Dominican Republic and Panama had been exhausted. The ship turned around, heading back toward Europe and probable death for the 937 refugees.

Gordon Thomas and Max Morgan Witts, who describe the incident in their book *Voyage of the Damned*, interviewed some of the few survivors of this journey. This is how the authors describe their reactions:

"A terrible personal realization touched each member of

the passenger committee. They dared not say so openly, even to each other. Some could not bear to mention it to their wives and children. It was inhuman, degrading and endured in private, but it cut deeply into one of their most basic human needs: the need to be wanted. Instead, they had been rejected. Even the New World did not want them; they now must again rely on the Old. The committee suffered in silence, knowing it was not just an anonymous group of people who had been turned down, but that they, individually, each one, had had an open door shut in their faces; through them, their entire race had been judged and found wanting. If some other country accepted them, they now believed it would be on sufferance."

And on sufferance it was. Realizing that these people would all be doomed to a terrible death if they were forced to return to Hamburg, a popular outcry finally arose in France, Belgium, Holland and Great Britain. Each of these countries agreed to accept some of the refugees, although under humiliating conditions. In Belgium they were herded into boarded-up rail-road cars and sent to an internment camp. In Antwerp there were some ugly scenes when a right-wing youth organization protested the arrival of the refugees. Handbills were distributed containing this message: "We, too, want to help the Jews. If they call at our offices, each will receive free-of-charge a length of rope and a long nail."

Only in France was their welcome friendly and encouraging. In England, most of the families were interned in camps as "enemy aliens," although eventually some of the men would volunteer for the British army and lose their lives in the war against their homeland.

As it turned out, only those who were allowed to land in England were relatively safe. Within a year, the Nazi armies had swept Holland, Belgium and France, and most of the refugees from the St. Louis found themselves part of Hitler's "final solution." Of the more than 900 people who returned to Europe, only 240 survived the war. "What is certain is that if

Cuba or the United States had opened their doors, almost no one from the ship need have died," the authors of *Voyage of the Damned* conclude.

So the answer to the German journalist's accusing question: "Where was everybody else?" is not a simple one. Certainly not everybody was willing to face the truth. Most people would have condemned what was happening in Germany had they known about it. But, as the journalist pointed out, the truth was more knowable in countries with a free press like the United States, than it was in a dictatorship where the press was controlled by the government and listening to foreign news broadcasts could mean death before a firing squad. But when the free press is the bearer of bad news, it is often simply not believed.

Nor was everybody eager to save others Hitler had put on his elimination lists. It was easier to refuse to believe what Hitler had spelled out quite clearly. Some countries allowed a small quota of Jews to emigrate. No one wanted Gypsies (who were also scheduled for extermination) or people who might be political troublemakers.

In looking at the world press and the history of most democratic societies during the crucial years of the late 1930s, it becomes evident that the answer implied in the German's question is at least partially true. Not everybody, but too many Americans and other citizens of the "free world" were at home minding their own business, ignoring the threatening headlines and reading the sports pages first. Many Germans were doing exactly the same thing.

As my German journalist friend pointed out early in our conversation, there is an enormous difference between misinterpreting an event and causing it. There is also a difference between committing a crime and turning away one's head when one is being committed.

Even with a free press (and perhaps because of it) "everybody else" may well have been confused. Confusion frequently results in nonaction. If one reads and hears different reports on the same events, one tends to take the most comfortable view, which is also often the most optimistic one. The bearers of bad tidings (in this case the most knowledgable and concerned reporters) are often accused of being troublemakers or even of somehow being responsible for the disasters they report.

Germans, even without a free press to tell them what was happening in their own country, had eyes and ears to see and hear. They knew, from firsthand experience, that their neighbors, friends, employers, employees, teachers, clergymen and former leaders were losing their livelihoods and disappearing without explanation. They heard and sometimes saw cattle cars filled with wretched men, women and children moving through their towns, even if these cars were usually timed to run only at night and placed on distant railroad sidings. Hitler was *their* leader, admired by most Germans until he began to cause misery to their own country instead of just to far-removed places like Czechoslovakia, Poland, Norway, France or Greece. The fact that a few citizens of these occupied countries collaborated with the Nazis as a means of survival, does not lessen the responsibility of those who allowed Hitler to come to power in the first place, even though they may have picked him in the name of law and order, or peace and patriotism.

As another German journalist put it: "The fact that many non-Germans were ignorant or irresponsible or even sympathetic to the Nazi movement doesn't excuse those of us who knew what was happening in our own country. Patriotism doesn't mean finding others to blame for one's own country's sins. It doesn't mean that you excuse blatant wrongs because they are done in the name of your country. The true patriots were the young people in the White Rose movement and others like them . . . who saw evil for what it was and tried to fight it, even when the fight sometimes seemed hopeless."

WHEN WILL THEY EVER LEARN?

"The quest for absolute possession is a threat to Man. Those who feel that they own the entire truth, those who will have the Paradise of their dreams here and now, destroy only too easily the ground on which a system allowing for human dignity can grow. The tradition of European democracy, too, knows not only of a humanitarian, but also of a doctrinaire trait, which leads to tyranny; liberation then becomes slavery.

"Young people often expect me to give an unqualified 'Yes,' a clear 'No.' But it has become impossible for me to believe in one, in the single truth, so I say to my young friends and to others who want to hear it: There are *several* truths, not merely the one truth which excludes all others. That is why I believe in diversity and hence in doubt. It is productive. It questions existing things. It can be strong enough to smash fossilized injustice. Doubt has proved its worth during the resistance. It is tough enough to outlast defeats and to disillusion victors."

—From the speech of thanks by Chancellor Willy Brandt of the Federal Republic of Germany at the ceremony awarding him the 1971 Nobel Prize for Peace in Oslo, December 10, 1971.

He resigned his office in May of 1974 because of a relatively minor political mistake (one of his aides turned out to be a Communist spy from Eastern Germany), taking the entire responsibility for the whole incident, and absolving any of his subordinates.

"AMERICA . . . LOVE IT OR LEAVE IT!"

—*A still popular automobile bumper sticker in the United States.*

". . . the present Government of the United States shows no concern for human rights. Henry Kissinger and his President were silent for months while their allies in Pakistan slaughtered the Bengalis. Washington has nothing to say about a Greek Government that rules by terror. Or about the Government of South Korea, whose kidnappings and brutalities make Communist regimes look almost decorous by comparison. (For a student to refuse to attend class in South Korea 'without plausible reasons' is a crime punishable by death.)

"Some of the nastiest governments in the world today were born or grew with American aid. That being the case, the most modest view of our responsibility would require us to say a restraining word to them occasionally. But we say nothing, we hear nothing, we see nothing."

—*Column by Anthony Lewis,* NEW YORK TIMES *May 31, 1974*

Where have all the soldiers gone? long time passing
Where have all the soldiers gone long time ago?
Where have all the soldiers gone?
They have gone to graveyards, everyone.
Oh, when will they ever learn?
Oh, when will they ever learn?

—*Words and music by Peter Seeger,*
additional verses by Joe Hickerson.

Willy Brandt was probably born a doubter. He was the illegitimate son of a German seamstress and never knew his father. Germans were always very straitlaced, and one can be almost certain that few people ever allowed him to forget the unconventional circumstances of his birth.

Nevertheless, he was able to enter one of the best high schools in his community, and shocked his schoolmates and teachers by wearing the Social Democratic Party's kerchief in a highly conservative setting.

After graduation he came under the influence of Julius Leber, a Social Democratic editor, who apparently replaced the father he had never known. With Leber's help he began to contribute articles to newspapers using not his real name (Herbert Ernst Karl Frahm), but the pen name Will Brandt (*Brandt* means "fire" in German). In 1933 he fled Germany and went to Norway. As a journalist, he covered the Spanish Civil War. The Germans caught up with him when they invaded Norway. Recognition would, of course, have meant certain death, but luckily they took him for just one more Norwegian soldier, and he spent only a few months in a prisoner of war camp. He escaped to Sweden in 1940, where he might have lived in complete safety. Instead he chose to go to Norway on several underground missions.

After the war he returned to Germany with a Norwegian citizenship and a press card. He worked briefly for the Norwegian military mission in Berlin, but in 1947 he resumed his German citizenship and his party membership in the Social Democrats. He was elected mayor of West Berlin in 1961; and when the Berlin Wall was constructed, he became one of the few mayors anywhere in the world whose name was indeed a household word.

In an interview a few days after the construction of the wall, I told him that many people regarded him as a "symbol of the free world." "I'm a symbol of nothing but myself," he said.

In subsequent interviews it was obvious that he never, for one second, confused the offices he held (which included the position of vice-chancellor and foreign minister) with himself as a person. Willy Brandt's wife was a working actress, and his sons tended to become involved in radical causes (which led to at least one arrest). This would have driven almost any other political figure into embarrassed explanations or spasms of rage. Brandt simply indicated that he expected his sons to act as individual, responsible human beings.

During one of his early election campaigns, I asked a close campaign associate whether Brandt had a chance of ever obtaining the top German government post. "I can't imagine an American politician who had, in a sense, fought with the enemy against his own country being elected dogcatcher," I remember telling the campaign aide. "You've been in the United States. Can you imagine my country electing someone who had fought for the Viet Cong as President?" "Germany is different now," the aide answered quietly. "You may not believe it, but Brandt is going to win. And one of the reasons for his victory will be his brief career in the Norwegian underground. Some Germans, especially some of our younger voters, admire him for that. They see him doing something that they wish their parents had done." So Brandt did become a symbol —even though he himself rejected the idea—a symbol of a Germany that felt it had learned something from its old mistakes.

Of course, there are many Germans who cannot forgive Brandt his past, and who want to excuse their own. A taxi driver in Munich cursed Brandt in some of the same language that New York taxi drivers frequently reserved for John Lindsay. Besides referring to him as "a Jew lover" (New York cabbies tend to concentrate their wrath on blacks and Puerto Ricans), he called him "a traitor" and then added: "After all, what can you expect from a bastard who doesn't even use his own name?" The same taxi driver also pointed out that while many of his American fares asked about Dachau, few wanted to know about all the good Hitler had done. "Who remembers the *Autobahn* [the superhighway] that he built?" he asked me grimly. "Who remembers that he reduced unemployment? Nobody, of course, the Jewish press sees to that." As we drove past the Loewenbrau beer brewery he said angrily: "This outfit, like most of Germany's best industries, belongs to a Jew. I think they need to be put down a notch or two again. Every Jew I know is a millionaire." I was just angry enough to tell him that although Jewish, I certainly didn't count myself among the superrich. As a matter of fact, I was so poor I couldn't afford a tip.

Another German woman, about my age, sat down at my table in a Berlin café. She looked like a caricature by George Grosz, overweight, grim-faced, and with one of those hunter's hats with little green feathers that are still worn in Germany by middle-aged women. Her wrath was directed at "hippies and Negroes who seem to have taken over our city." She grew red with rage every time she saw one or more blacks (often students at the Free University in Berlin) passing, laughing and joking. "Too bad we got rid of the concentration camps," she said. "Of course, I wouldn't want to starve or gas anybody to death, but these bums ought to be taken off the streets. One is afraid to go out alone, even in the afternoon." I pointed out that she was out, alone, in the afternoon, and that nobody seemed to be bothering her. I also remarked that her statement reminded me a great deal of what I had heard in 1936; and then the remarks had been directed at *me*. She had the good grace to blush and leave the table we shared.

On a train from Frankfurt to Munich I kept meeting men and women who assured me that the stories about the concentration camps had all been lies. And even if there was a grain of truth in them, what about the Allies fire bombing Dresden that had killed thousands of people? What about the atom bombs? What about the Israelis who drove thousands of Arabs from their homes?

Since I speak fluent German, and with the help of a pair of German-made shoes and a session in a German beauty parlor, can hide any trace of my American education and life, I could observe that people spoke differently to me when they thought I was just another German, than when I clearly identified myself as an American reporter. There was less humility, less regret, more snide references to Jews, blacks and other minority groups, and more praise of "the good things Hitler had done," when I appeared as a German than when I used my American identity. I was occasionally attacked as "un-German" or even "a traitor to the fatherland" when I objected or argued. However, none of this happened when I was talking to anyone under thirty. Most of Germany's young people seem to be critical of the past, to talk about it, regret it and try to find reasons for Hitler's rise to power in order that the past will not repeat itself. Whether I appeared as a German or as an American, there seemed to be little doubt in the minds of the young people I met: the atrocities that had occurred in the 1930s and forties must never happen again; not in Germany nor anywhere else. However, many of these young people might have benefited by Brandt's advice to maintain a healthy cynicism. Some of them had instant solutions, ranging from orthodox Marxism, to Maoism, to any number of other forms of absolute truths for all the world's problems. In that, they were no different from young men and women in the United States and elsewhere. To many of them, doubt is still a dirty word.

In a high-school classroom in West Berlin I was quizzed about my own past. "Why did you leave?" one of the students asked. "Why didn't you stay and fight?" "If you had stayed, what would you have done?" "Would you have risked your life to oppose what you knew to be evil?" In all honesty, I had to tell the students that I simply didn't have answers to their questions. Who knows what he or she would do under conditions of extreme stress? They had obviously asked their own parents why conditions such as the Nuremberg Laws and the concentration camps had been tolerated. The answers they had received had apparently been unsatisfactory. In a way, so were mine. The generation gap in Germany often seems more like a chasm—unbridgeable by all but a few.

During my latest trip to Germany, some of the conversations began taking a slightly different turn. "What has the rest of the world learned from our experience?" was one of the most frequently asked questions. Often the speaker answered his own query: "Nothing at all, it seems." The fact that thousands of political prisoners were being tortured and killed in Chile and Greece was frequently mentioned. "Your country supports those fascist regimes, even gives them arms and money." The fact that Jews in Russia, Syria, Iraq, Argentina and other places were persecuted and that America seemed to be more interested in trade and influence in these countries than in the fate of the same minority that had suffered such desperate wrongs under Hitler, was frequently mentioned. Always by young people who could not feel any personal responsibility for what had happened in their own country before they were born.

One student showed me a paper he had done on Lord Acton, pointing out that the British nobleman's grandfather had been a Bavarian duke. In the paper there was a quote he urged me to copy: "The inflexible integrity of the moral code is to me the secret of authority, the dignity, the utility of history. If we debase it for the sake of a man's influence, of his religion, of his party, of the good cause which prospers his credit and suffers his disgrace, then History ceases to be a science, an arbiter of controversy, a guide to the wanderer . . . It serves where it ought to reign, and it serves the worst cause better than the purest. . . . If the high be criminal, then the authority permitting it bears the guilt . . . Power tends to corrupt and absolute power corrupts absolutely."

After I had read the very intelligent paper, I didn't have to wait long for the expected question: "What about your Watergate?" Telling young Germans that Nixon is not Hitler, that Watergate is not an equivalent of Hitler's acts of mind and thought control, turned out not to be a very good answer.

Actually, for young Germans and young Americans, who increasingly question the ability of *any* government to govern fairly, justly and honestly, there are no answers, except the one that Willy Brandt outlined in his Nobel Prize speech. In the arena of government blind faith is dangerous. "My country right or wrong" is a statement that a great many Germans made, until their government disappeared from the face of the earth. It's a statement that many Americans still regard as the essence of patriotism.

Looking at the history of my former homeland, Germany, and my new country, the United States, I have remembered, over and over again, the words of the strong and marvelous old German teacher and editor, Annedore Leber. She was the widow of Julius Leber, who had taken Willy Brandt under his wing and to whom he probably owes many of his ideas and principles. Frau Leber suffered horribly under the Nazi regime. Her husband was one of the first Germans arrested and thrown into a concentration camp. For years she didn't know whether he was alive or not. She supported herself and her two children by doing housework, sewing at night—anything and everything necessary for survival, except renouncing her husband and his principles. Had she agreed to do this, she could have resumed her professional career and lived in relative comfort instead of on the edge of starvation and in constant danger to her own life. Julius Leber was released from his incarceration long enough to join the plot against Hitler's life. At his trial he denied neither his beliefs nor his actions. He was executed.

Frau Leber established a publishing house after the war. Her purpose was to publish books for young people, to remind them not only of the horrors of the Nazi era, but of those few whose consciences did not allow them to remain silent and who paid with their lives. "Are you trying to help your country regain its self-respect?" I asked her once. "What do you mean by 'country'?" she asked in return. "Look around you at the German countryside. Does it seem different from what it was when you left in 1936? Look at the people. Do they look different? Probably not, but we *are* different, although technically, we are still the same country. The people who live here, their ideas, their feelings, the sense of decency and rectitude that *they* must impart to their government is really what a country is all about. That's true for us . . . and for you. When you start believing that morality or immorality filters down from the top instead of up from the bottom, you've lost your country already."

I asked her whether she felt that her own fight had been worth all her suffering. "Definitely," she answered. Two years later her beloved son, whose life had been blighted by the Hitler years, committed suicide. She was asked by another reporter whether she still considered her sacrifices worthwhile. "Sometimes I doubt it now," she said. But that was a momentary weakness. During a telephone conversation a few months later, she mentioned that interview. "Of course, anyone can reach the point of desperation," she said, "but, yes, I still believe that those few who like my husband fought the government because they loved their country did the right thing . . . no matter what it cost."

So perhaps, in Germany and in many other countries, including our own, democracy can never really fail. Among those who have known freedom, who believe in the dignity of all human beings (including their own), there will always be those who like the Scholls, like Julius and Annedore Leber, like Rosie, Klaus and Minna, and all those others who told their stories for this book, who will help a faltering democracy to regain its perspective and rise again, even out of a holocaust like Hitler's Thousand Year Reich, that actually lasted only twelve years.

Index

Abitur (German High School examination), 63, 64, 65
Academy of Fine Arts, Vienna, 57
Acton, Lord, 167
Adolescents, German (attitudes toward Nazis), 62–74
Agnew, Spiro, 155
Alsace-Lorraine, 18
Arabs, 165
Aristocracy, German, 49, 88
Article 48 Weimar Constitution, 24, 25, 49
Artists and Musicians (attitudes toward Hitler), 121–22
Aryans, 90, 91, 142, 143, 147
Attitudes of today's young Germans, toward the past, 166
Auden, W. H., 3
Austria, 61
Autobahn, 164

Auxiliary Military Service, 128

Bavaria, 5, 67
Berlin, 3, 6, 10, 12, 16, 20, 21, 47, 64, 70, 93, 119, 144, 151
Bill of Rights, 25
"Blowin' in the Wind," 119
Bolshevism, 23
Book burning, 80–81
Branau-Am-Inn, 55
Brandenburg Gate, 6
Brandt, Willy, 161–64, 166, 168
Brecht, Berthold, 64, 112
Brownshirts, 6, 51, 127
Bruening, Heinrich, 48, 49, 51
Budzinski, Klaus, *ix*
Bund Deutsche Maedeln, 6

Cabaret (film and play), 21, 88–89
CBS, 155
Chairman Mao, 60
Chandler, Douglas, 149

Chasins, Abraham, 44
Chicago Tribune, 155
Chile, 167
Civic Disorder, 88
Civil Liberties,
    sacrifice of, 85
    suppression of press, etc.,
    82–84
Communists and Commu-
    nism in Germany, 24, 47,
    49, 78, 139, 153, 155
Compiègne, Forest of, 17
Concentration camps, 92, 131–
    36, 165
Construction workers, U.S.,
    attack on students, 117
Constitution, German
    (present), 26
Constitution, U.S., 22, 26
Constitution, Weimar Repub-
    lic, 9, 22, 77
Coughlin, William
    (Father), 153
Cuba, 156

Dachau, concentration camp,
    26, 132, 164
    museum of, 134
    town of, 131–33
*Das Haus der Deutschen
    Kunst* (The House of
    German Art), 81, 82
Denmark, King of, 145
Dresden, fire bombing of, 165
Dylan, Bob, 119

Eastern Establishment Press,
    155

East Prussia, 6, 69
Ebb, Fred, 87
Ebert, Friederich, 11–14, 16,
    19, 24
Education in German High
    School, 63–64
Emigration of Jews, 156–58
Erzberger, Mattias, 17, 19
Essen, 16, 83, 130
"Exhibition of Forbidden
    Art," 82

Feuermann, Emanuel, 52
Forchtenberg, 127
Fazit, 98–99
France, 18
Frahm, Herber, Ernst, Karl
    (real name of Willy
    Brandt), 19, 63
Frankfurt, 12, 65
Frank, Hans, 137
*Frankfurter Allgemeine Zei-
    tung* (liberal newspaper),
    71
Frederick the Great, 59, 79
Free Press, 159–60
Free University in Berlin, 165
Freikorps, 23, 24
Friedrich, Otto, 10, 29, 44, 52
Fritsch, Theodore, 4
From the Diary of a Snail,
    116–17
Frost, Robert, 62

Generation gap in Germany,
    166
German Empire, 10, 12
German Republic, 3, 10, 13

Goebbels, Joseph, 46–47, 81–
82, 157
Goering, Hermann, 50, 72
"Good Germans" attitudes
toward Nazis, 121–23
Graf, Willi, 129
Grass, Günter, 116
Greece, 167
Grosz, George, 27, 29, 30, 31

Hamburg, 156, 157
Hanke, Karl, 131
Heine, Heinrich, 79
Himmler, Heinrich, 132
"Hippies," 165
Hitler, Adolf, *viii*, 4, 10, 19,
53–62, 93, 167,
anti-Semitism, reasons for,
56–57
artistic ambitions, 56–57
attention-getting devices,
94–95
becomes Chancellor, 52
feeling About Weimar
Constitution, 25
how financed, 50
idealized by the young, 74
physical appearance, 59
plot to kill, 60
reasons for rise to power, 31,
46, 51, 60–61
service in World War I, 57
standard speech, 95–96
taste in art and literature, 81
taste in music, 121
Hitler years, *viii, ix*
Hitler Youth Movement, 7, 8,
20–21, 70, 72–73, 85, 88,

91, 97, 119–20, 126–27,
132
Songbook, 87–88, 126
Hohler, Ali, 47, 50
Holocaust, 137–48
Horst Wessel Song (official
Nazi anthem), 47, 150
Huber, Kurt, 129
Hughes, Michael, 54

Idealists (Nazi), 89–90
Immigration quotas, 156
Imperial Palace, 11
Industrialist, German, 49, 60
Inflation, 27–31, 45
Inside the Third Reich, 16
Intellectuals, 16, 52, 82, 115
Isherwood, Christopher, 44
Israelis, 165

Jesus movement, *vii*
Jewish Community Center
(Berlin), 143, 147
Jews, 4, 5, 97
German attitudes toward,
120–21, 136
hatred of, 45, 46, 69–70
in Russia, Syria, Iraq,
Argentina, 167
Johnson, Lyndon B., *viii*
Joint Distribution Committee,
157
Journalists, 16

Kaiser, 10, 11, 12, 18
Keller, Helen, 81
Kennedy, John F., *vii*
Kennedy, Robert, *vii*

Kent State University, *vii*
King, Martin Luther, Jr., *vii*
Klee, Paul, 82
Kristallnacht (night of glass),
  144

Langer, William C. (Dr.), 52
"Law and order," 26
League of Nations, 18
Leber, Annedore, 168–69
Leber, Julius, 168
Lewis, Anthony, 162
Liberals, 46, 73
  Hitler's attitude toward, 50
  Liberal press, 45
Liebknecht, Karl, 10, 11, 12,
  23
Lindbergh, Anne Morrow, 153,
  154
Lindbergh, Charles, 153
Lindsay, John, 164
Loewenbrau, 165
London, 7
London, Jack, 81
Luxemburg, Rosa, 24

Mahagonny (German political
  musical), 112–14
Maoism, 166
Marxism, 50, 166
  Hitler's attitude toward
  Marx as a Jew, 50
Maschmann, Melita, 98–99
Mein Kampf, 18, 76
Mischling (someone of mixed
  blood), 143, 146, 147
Morrow, William, 153
Mueller, Hermann, 48

Munich, *ix*, 47, 93, 133, 164–65
Murrow, Edward R., 155
My Lai, *vii*, 119, 123

National Archives, 122
National Geographic, 149,
  150, 151, 152
Nazi Party, *viii*, 26, 49, 52, 140
  early activities, 78
  women's movement, 85
  spying on German citizens,
  84
NBC, 155
Neukoeln, 47
New York Post, 155
New York Times, 155, 162
Nixon, Richard M., *viii*, 167
North Dakota, 81
Nuremberg Laws, 142, 166
  trial, 16

"Old Shatterhand" (in Karl
  May's novels), 56
Olympic Games (1936), 141

Philadelphia, 23
Picasso, Pablo, 82
"Pied Piper of Hamelin," 126
Poland, 18
  Polish Corridor, 18
Pornography, 82
Posen, 18
Preuss, Hugo, 25
Probst, Christopher, 129
Provincial States, German, 23
Prussians, 67

Reader's Digest, 153

Reichsbank, 29
Reichstag, 10, 49, 61
  dissolution of, 51
  fire, 78
  Nazi seats in, 51–52
  present, 61
Reparations, 18
Revolution, 10, 11, 16, 28, 50
Rhineland, 61
Romantic tradition, German,
  58
Roosevelt, Franklin D., 153
Rotterdam, 7

Saar District, 18
St. Louis (refugee ship), 156–
  58
Sanger, Margaret, 81
Scheidemann, Phillip, 11
Schickelgruber, Adolf, 55
Schnorrell, Alexander, 129
Scholls, the, 169
  Hans, 8, 124
  Inge, 8, 125–30
  Sophie, 8, 125–30
School system, German
  (*Gymnasium* and *Real-
  schule*), 55
Shirer, William C., 155
Social Democratic Party, 52,
  163
Socialists, 5, 13, 47, 50, 67
Soviets, 11
Spartakists, 23
Speer, Albert, 15, 16, 53, 131
Splinter parties, 51, 52
State Labor Service, 128
"States Rights," 23

States, U.S., 23
Street Battles, attitude of
  police, 93–94, 96, 97
Swastika, 21
Swiss attitudes toward Jewish
  refugees, 156

Tent cities, 46
Theater, German (1930–33),
  64
Third Reich, 4
Thomas, Gordon, 157
Thompson, Dorothy, 155
Thousand Year Reich, 74, 169
Time, 119
"Tomorrow Belongs to Me,"
  87, 88, 92

Ullstein newspapers, 29
Unemployment, 13, 45–46, 69
University of Munich, 8, 124,
  128
Upper Silesia, 18

Values, German, 115
Versailles treaty, 63, 72
Vietcong, 164
Vietnam, 119, 123, 136
Voelkischer Beobachter, 71,
  93, 132
Vonnegut, Kurt, 81
Von Baden, Max (Prince), 11
Von Hindenburg, Paul, 13, 17,
  48, 78
Von Richthofen, Baron, 72
Voyage of the Damned, 157

Watergate, 119, 123, 167

The Wave of the Future: A Confession of Faith, 153
Weathermen, *vii*
Weil, Kurt, 112
Weimar Republic, *viii,* 16, 23, 26, 51, 89, 93, 122, 155
Wertheim's, 5
Wessel, Horst, 47, 50
West Berlin, 163, 166

"White Rose," 8, 9, 124–30, 160
Witts, Max M., 157
World War I, 16, 45, 63, 72, 132
World War II, *viii,* 13, 21, 48, 61, 128, 145

Yellow star, 145
Young Americans for Freedom, *vii*